Share, Don't Take the Lead

Leadership Lessons from 21 Vanguard Organizations

AUTHORS' PREVIOUS BOOKS

Books by Pearce

The Drucker Difference
Craig L. Pearce, Joseph Maciariello and Hideki Yamawaki
(McGraw-Hill, 2010)

Shared Leadership: Reframing the Hows and Whys of Leadership
Craig L. Pearce and Jay A. Conger
(Sage Publications, 2003)

Books by Manz

Mastering Self-Leadership: Empowering Yourself for Personal Excellence
Charles C. Manz
(Prentice-Hall Press, 1992; with Christopher P. Neck: 2nd ed., 1999;
3rd ed., 2004; 4th ed., 2007; 5th ed., 2010; 6th edition, 2013)

Fit to Lead: The Proven Solution for Shaping up Your Body, Mind, and Career
Christopher P. Neck, Tedd L. Mitchell, Charles C. Manz,
Emmett C. Thompson, II and Janet Tornelli-Mitchell
(Carpenter's Son Publishing, 2012)

The Leadership Wisdom of Jesus: Practical Lessons For Today
Charles C. Manz
(Berrett-Koehler, 1998; soft-cover 1999; 2nd ed., 2005; 3rd ed., 2011)

*The Virtuous Organization: Lessons From Some of the World's Leading
Management Thinkers*
Charles C. Manz, Kim Cameron, Karen P. Manz, Robert D. Marx (Eds.)
(World Scientific Publishers, 2008)

Nice Guys Can Get the Corner Office:
Eight Strategies for Winning in Business Without Being a Jerk
Russ Edleman, Tim Hiltabiddle, and Charles C. Manz
(Penguin, 2008)

The Greatest Leader Who Wasn't: A Leadership Fable
Charles C. Manz
(Walk the Talk Publishers, 2005)

Temporary Sanity: Instant Self-Leadership Strategies for Turbulent Times
Charles C. Manz
(Financial Times Prentice-Hall, 2005)

*Fit to Lead: The Proven 8-Week Solution for Shaping up Your Body,
Your Mind, and Your Career*
Christopher P. Neck, Tedd L. Mitchell, Charles C. Manz,
and Emmett C. Thompson, II
(St. Martin's Press, 2004)

The Power to Choose How You Feel (Short book format)
Charles C. Manz
(Successories, 2004)

Emotional Discipline: The Power to Choose How You Feel
Charles C. Manz
(Berrett-Koehler, 2003)

The Power of Failure: 27 Ways to Turn Life's Setbacks into Success
Charles C. Manz
(Berrett-Koehler, 2002)

The Wisdom of Solomon at Work: Ancient Virtues for Living and Leading Today
Charles C. Manz, Karen P. Manz, Robert D. Marx and Christopher P. Neck
(Berrett-Koehler, 2001)

*For Team Members Only: Making Your Workplace Team Productive
and Hassle-Free*
Charles C. Manz, Christopher P. Neck, James Mancuso, and Karen P. Manz
(AMACOM, 1997)

Self-Leadership: A Skill Building Series
A set of 3 workbooks including:
1) "Becoming a Self-Manager: Skills for Addressing Difficult,
Unattractive, but Necessary Tasks"
2) "Redesigning the Way you Do Your Job: Skills for Building
Natural Motivation Into Your Work"
3) The Art of Positive Psyching: Skills for Establishing
Constructive Thinking Patterns"
Charles C. Manz
(Organization Design and Development, 1993)

*The Art of Self-Leadership: Strategies for Personal Effectiveness
in Your Life and Work*
Charles C. Manz
(Prentice-Hall, 1983)

Books by Sims

The New Leadership Paradigm
Henry P. Sims, Jr. and Peter Lorenzi
(Sage Publications, 1992)

The Thinking Organization
Henry P. Sims, Jr. and Dennis Gioia
(Jossey Bass, 1986)

Books by Manz and Sims

The New SuperLeadership: Leading Others to Lead Themselves
Charles C. Manz and Henry P. Sims, Jr.
(Berrett-Koehler, 2001)

Team Work and Group Dynamics
Gregory Stewart, Charles C. Manz, and Henry P. Sims, Jr.
(Wiley, 1999)

Company of Heroes: Unleashing the Power of Self-Leadership
Henry P. Sims, Jr. and Charles C. Manz
(Wiley, 1996)

*Business Without Bosses: How Self-Managing Teams Are Building
High Performance Companies*
Charles C. Manz and Henry P. Sims, Jr.
(Wiley, 1993; soft-cover 1995)

SuperLeadership: Leading Others to Lead Themselves
Charles C. Manz and Henry P. Sims, Jr.
(Prentice-Hall, 1989; soft-cover, Berkley Books, 1990)

Share, Don't Take the Lead

Leadership Lessons from 21 Vanguard Organizations

Craig L. Pearce
Charles C. Manz
Henry P. Sims, Jr.

INFORMATION AGE PUBLISHING, INC.
Charlotte, NC • www.infoagepub.com

Library of Congress Cataloging-in-Publication Data

A CIP record for this book is available from the Library of Congress
http://www.loc.gov

ISBN: 978-1-62396-475-7 (Paperback)
        978-1-62396-476-4 (Hardcover)
        978-1-62396-477-1 (ebook)

CONTENTS

SECTION III
DISTRIBUTED SHARED LEADERSHIP

SECTION IV
COMPREHENSIVE SHARED LEADERSHIP

ACKNOWLEDGEMENTS

First, we would like to acknowledge our consorts, two of whom are contributors to this book, for their support and encouragement throughout the process of developing this book. In turn, they are Christina L. Wassenaar, Karen Manz, and Laurie Sims. This book project, as most, took longer than expected and we want to thank the team at Information Age Publishing for their encouragement. Naturally, there were many other players in the game. We would, for example, like to recognize the support of our universities in making this book possible. In the case of Craig L. Pearce this means thanks go to the Peter F. Drucker and Masatoshi Ito School of Management at Claremont Graduate University, the University of Nebraska-Lincoln, the American University of Nigeria and Ozyegin University. In the case of Charles C. Manz thanks go to the Isenberg School of Management at the University of Massachusetts–Amherst and in the case of Henry P. Sims, Jr. thanks go to the Robert H. Smith School of Business at the University of Maryland-College Park. Special thanks are due to Judith Yargawa at American University of Nigeria. Finally, we wish to thank the organizations and individuals who helped to inspire the creation of this book by sharing the lead so effectively.

INTRODUCTION TO SHARED LEADERSHIP

Craig L. Pearce and Charles C. Manz

Our world is at a leadership tipping point. The three powerful Cs of *complexity, change,* and *competition,* from around the globe, call for a new more potent and robust form of leadership...one that truly taps the capacity, experience and creativity of the entire workforce. This book describes just such a form of leadership that we believe answers this call and that represents the most effective practical leadership approach available for meeting today's organizational challenges—Shared Leadership. Shared leadership is a comprehensive term and it encompasses all aspects of leadership. To wit, all leadership is shared leadership, it is simply a matter of degree—sometimes it is shared completely while at other times it is not shared at all. But when it is truly shared across behavioral influence approaches; across structural boundaries; and across organizational forms, the results—from our decades of research—demonstrate profoundly positive organizational outcomes. At its most extreme, shared leadership is just what it sounds like: It means involving social actors in the process of leading one another toward productive ends. Thus, it moves beyond the moribund myth of leadership being a solely top-down hierarchical affair into a dynamic give and take relationship.

Shared leadership is a philosophical perspective on leadership. There are scads of other terms bandied about regarding leadership—charismatic

Share, Don't Take the Lead, pages xi–xix
Copyright © 2014 by Information Age Publishing
All rights of reproduction in any form reserved.

leadership, conventional leadership, collective leadership, distributed leadership, empowering leadership, rotated leadership, strategic leadership, servant leadership, team leadership, and visionary leadership—to name just a few. The cynical view is that most of these labels are related and are coined just to carve out shelf space for books, just as consumer goods brand managers do for the umpteenth type of soap to sell at the supermarket. Shared leadership, however, is a little bit different. Shared leadership encompasses these other terms and provides a way of organizing and making sense of them (See Figure I.1).

Shared leadership is not simply some technique to be foisted on employees as a new flavor of the month like so many managerial initiatives instigated by supposed thought leaders and opinion makers. Rather, the

Shared Leadership

The all encompassing leadership concept that incorporates: (1) structural forms; (2) influence approaches; and (3) organizational levels

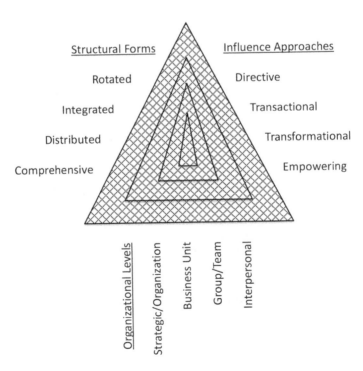

Figure I.1 Shared leadership.

philosophy of shared leadership rests on the notion that nearly every single human being is capable of sharing the burden and responsibility of leading, at least to some extent, in nearly all types of organizational circumstances. Naturally, this flies in the face of conventional wisdom extolled by self-proclaimed management gurus, who provide simple formulaic so-called solutions to cure all organizational woes. Consumers of such managerial prescriptions need to beware of simple solutions. People and organizations are complex. As such, organizational solutions need to be tailored to organizational realities: Realities like, What are the key internal challenges we face? What is the status of our talent pool? What are the likely threats and opportunities on the horizon? What is the state of the economy? What are our direct competitors planning? What unknown future competition might we face? How do we attract and retain the right talent? What products and service lines should we abandon? How might abandonment affect the talent we need? Should we partner with outsiders? If so, how? And responding to these and many other key questions is merely the beginning point for addressing how one should consider the development of appropriate shared leadership. In truth, nearly all organizations practice some form of shared leadership, whether they desire it or not.

Some of the terms presented above refer to the *context* within which leadership is exerted (e.g., strategic leadership, team leadership). Others refer to how leadership *influence* is exerted (e.g., transformational leadership, empowering leadership) while others refer to the *structural form* of leadership (e.g., distributed leadership, rotated leadership) of these three ways of thinking about leadership—*context, influence, form*—context is the most simplistic. In other words, context is simply where leadership takes place—the other dimensions are more interesting. Thus, we will not delve into the context too deeply here. Rather, below we will first examine four fundamental influence approaches to leadership. Then, we will examine four fundamental structural forms of shared leadership—which serve to organize the chapters of this book. We will then turn our attention to what actions you, as a hierarchical leader, can take to encourage and foster appropriate shared leadership in your organization.

THE KEY TYPES OF LEADERSHIP INFLUENCE

It is important to know, based on scientific research, that shared leadership positively impacts organizational outcomes. It is critical to understand the specific behavioral approaches involved in sharing leadership. Accordingly, below we identify four specific behavioral processes needed to effectively practice shared leadership. In the following section we then examine some specific practices needed from hierarchical leaders to support the ongoing development of effective shared leadership. We subsequently identify different idiosyncratic forms of shared leadership we found through our research in the many different organizations we studied. Then, in the rest of this book we dive deep into the stories of several organizations that are at the cutting edge of shared leadership and attempt to extract leadership lessons that you can take back to your organization.

Our author team has conducted decades of research on leadership and we have identified a range of leadership strategies or behaviors that serve as the bases of influence between leaders and followers. Our early work has focused more on hierarchical leaders but we have found that in the context of shared leadership, these strategies continue to be relevant, with one important caveat: The agents and targets of influence are often peers. Our research has identified four fundamental types of leadership behavior that a person can use to influence others:

1. Directive
2. Transactional
3. Transformational
4. Empowering

Below, we articulate each of these specific behavioral approaches in more detail.

Directive Leadership

Directive leadership involves providing task focused directions, instructions or recommendations. Directive leadership, for example, can help provide much-needed structure for unstructured tasks. Highly skilled workers, be they hierarchical leaders or other members of an organization, generally find a receptive audience among less-experienced or less-knowledgeable members for well-meaning and constructive prescription and direction. Directive leadership is particularly important in newly formed or recently re-formed teams, for instance. Shared directive leadership might also be expressed in conversation as peers test each other with a directive give and take about how to allocate roles, approach assignments, or resolve conflicting points of view on task relevant issues. Indeed, task conflict (disagreement about how to perform work), as defined by social scientists, is highly related to shared directive leadership and has been positively linked to performance in a wide variety of contexts, including the financial performance of firms.

Transactional Leadership

Transactional leadership is another way to influence people. It involves strategically providing valued rewards—praise, compensation, or other desirable outcomes—contingent on behavior or performance. Typically, the organizational source of such rewards has been an appointed, hierarchical leader. However, shared transactional leadership can, for example, be expressed with collegial praise for being a good organizational citizen. Colleagues can also dynamically cover for one another based on who has garnered such support through previous performance. In extreme cases, colleagues can even recommend financial distributions based on individual- or team- level attainment of milestones or other performance metrics, which we have seen in action in one of the firms in our research. Naturally, team-based pay leads to positive team outcomes. These are but a few of the ways transactional leadership practices can be deployed and shared in organizations. Again, we delve deeper into the actual enactment of shared transactional leadership in the subsequent chapters of this book.

Transformational Leadership

While transactional leadership emphasizes rewards of more-or-less immediate value, transformational leadership centers on a more inspirational emphasis on commitment to an overarching vision or mission. Most of the popular books on leadership claim how important it is for formal leaders to be inspirational and visionary (and we do not dispute this). Nevertheless, one thing that became very clear from our research is that it is the *sharing* of the visioning process that has a profoundly greater impact on a wide array of organizational outcomes. For example, we found sharing vision creation to positively impact how altruistic people are to one another; to the level of courtesy displayed in organizations; to the amount of teamwork in which people engage; to the amount of resiliency people have in the face of adversity; and yes, strongly, to performance. Sharing transformational leadership helps people focus on fulfilling higher order needs, such as deriving meaning from one's work. We hope the subsequent stories in this book help to inspire you on how to share the inspiration with others.

Empowering Leadership

The fourth type of leadership behavior we advocate is empowering leadership, which emphasizes how people can engage in self-influence rather than simply relying on influence from others. Empowering leadership is an essential role of the designated, hierarchical leader if those below him or her are to effectively share leadership. Just like the other leadership behaviors discussed above, empowering leadership can also be shared and projected laterally among peers. Examples of shared empowering leadership include peer encouragement and support of self-goal-setting, self-evaluation, self-reward and self-development. Shared empowering leadership emphasizes building self-influence skills that preserve autonomy, while encouraging orchestration of performance with the larger collective. Empowering leadership is, in fact, the cornerstone of shared leadership: Without empowering leadership from above, shared leadership is, at best, wishful thinking.

FORMS OF SHARED LEADERSHIP

Shared leadership is not a one size fits all type of concept. From our investigation, we identified four distinct types of shared leadership in organizations—rotated, integrated, distributed and comprehensive. Accordingly, our book is organized into sections for each of these types.

Rotated Shared Leadership

Rotated shared leadership, as the term suggests, involves conscious strategies to have different people clearly assuming the role of leader at different points in time. This might be as simple as someone agreeing to be team leader for a certain term with the understanding that the role will rotate to different members of the group at different points in time. Alternatively, it might involve leadership transitions a bit more quickly, such as following Robert's Rules of Order for meetings where specific rules dictate when and how a person gets to "take the floor" for a period of time. The examples in this book, however, are a bit more dramatic. The first is drawn from Alcoholics Anonymous (AA). AA is a completely volunteer organization and is one of the most hyper-altruistic organizations on earth. If for-profit organizations could learn just a small percentage of the leadership lessons from AA the world would indeed be a better place. The second example of rotated shared leadership examines the University of Maryland Trauma Center, where they deal with major crises, while teaching novice doctors to become experts. Leadership is rotated depending on the severity of the cases and the experience levels of the doctors involved. It is a fascinating case that dramatically illustrates how to transfer leadership responsibility over time.

Integrated Shared Leadership

Integrated shared leadership is a bit more dynamic than rotated shared leadership, where leadership roles shift and transition more fluidly and rapidly between the individuals involved. The organizations we examine here include Palm Pilot and Smartphone and Southwestern Airlines. In the chapter on Palm Pilot and Smart Phone we examine a small top management team that started up the business that created the Palm Pilot and subsequently another business (Handspring) that introduced the Smart Phone. These talented professionals combined their distinct expertise in the areas of technology, marketing and executive management. A dynamic, high-performance shared leadership approach resulted that produced two highly successful organizations (subsequently, Palm Pilot purchased Handspring forming one company). This case stands as a notable example of what an entrepreneurial team can accomplish when its members share in the leadership process.

Southwest Airlines illustrates a keen example of integrated shared leadership. If you invested $10,000 in the fledgling Southwest Airlines in 1972 your retirement would be set. Today, that investment would be worth well over 10 million dollars. What is behind Southwest's impressive financial record? For one thing, Southwest Airlines is one of the most admired companies in the United States, number seven according to the 2013 *Fortune* magazine rating. This is not a fluke rating. Southwest is consistently in the top ten. Ironically, however, and contrary to the advice of pop-marketing books, they achieve this by not focusing on the customer. Rather, Southwest achieves this by focusing on their employees, or in Southwest parlance, focusing on their co-workers. What's their secret? According to Jim Parker, former CEO of Southwest, "Many people think that the source of our success is our pay structure—that we pay our people less than our competitors—but that simply isn't true. The real source of our competitive advantage is our culture, which is based firmly on the principles of distributed and shared leadership."

Distributed Shared Leadership

Distributed shared leadership, in contrast, deals more with how to disperse leadership roles widely in an organization. The examples explored in this section include the redevelopment of the educational system in Afghanistan, a sampling of megachurches, and Alcoa's experience in developing parallel global virtual teams.

Much of this book focuses on organizations using shared leadership that are primarily located in the west and the United States, specifically.

Nevertheless, shared leadership has enabled dramatic leadership change to occur in a variety of places around the globe. Here, we will briefly describe how School Management Committees (SMCs) in Afghanistan have enabled shared leadership to flourish for a radical shift in the leadership and governance of the country's education system to occur.

Megachurches and their high-profile singular charismatic leaders seem to go hand in hand. In fact, the image is so strong that they are often accused of being "cults of personality," religious enterprises resting on the shoulders of a "great man" theory of spiritual leadership. This isn't too surprising given the national prominence of megachurch pastors such as Rick Warren at Saddleback Church, Lake Forest, CA; Joel Osteen of Lakewood Church, Houston, TX; or Bill Hybels of Willow Creek Community Church, South Barrington, IL. Nevertheless, a closer look at the style of leadership practiced in many megachurches that are more successful over the long term reveals a different story. In fact, we find significant empowerment, particularly at the senior staff level, encouraging motivation based on people discovering their special gifts, and a team leadership approach to living out each person's special capacities and interests within the broad structure of the church's well-defined vision and mission.

Parallel global virtual teams represent a relatively new organizational response to the complexities and challenges of the modern world. Alcoa is a pioneer in this space. To be successful they need to rely on a form of shared leadership that spans organizational and geographical boundaries and operates outside the formal organizational authority structure. Their approach offers considerable potential advantages for organizations seeking to leverage diverse and dispersed expertise. The Alcoa experience is a vivid example of how non-traditional organizational structures can be utilized to enhance organization-wide distributed shared leadership.

Comprehensive Shared Leadership

In our final section we explore three companies that practice comprehensive shared leadership—they infuse shared leadership practices throughout their entire cultures. These three firms are Herman Miller, W. L. Gore & Associates, and the owner of the famous Panda Express restaurant chain—Panda Restaurant Group.

Herman Miller, Inc. originated as a home furniture maker more than a century ago, and has been an innovative leader in the office furniture industry since the 1940s. The company has a long tradition of shared leadership. This chapter shows how the company sustained a culture of shared leadership during:

1. The company's transition to non-family members and then to outsiders as top management in the 1980s and 1990s
2. The company's crisis after the dotcom meltdown, when the company's revenue levels fell by a third in 2002

W. L. Gore & Associates is a company that has practiced shared leadership without formal structures for 50 years. For the first 40 or more years, leaders developed teams in their local plants. Plants were kept to 200 employees to facilitate team development. As the business has become increasingly global, virtual teams have replaced within-plant teams. Members are distributed frequently across multiple countries and continents. Maintaining shared leadership and facilitating the development of new leaders across geographical and cultural hurdles presents the greatest challenge to Gore according to its President and CEO Terri Kelly. This chapter focuses on how that challenge evolved and how it is being met.

Panda's stated mission is to "Deliver exceptional Asian dining experiences by building an organization where people are inspired to better their lives." And they mean it. Panda is very purposeful about developing shared leadership. One mechanism they use involves creating temporary cross-functional teams to tackle important organizational issues as part of its custom executive education program for rising stars. They have more than quadrupled in size in the past decade and currently have more than 1,600 locations. Accordingly, this chapter focuses on how to infuse shared leadership throughout an entire culture to drive high growth.

THE ROLE OF HIERARCHICAL LEADERS IN THE ONGOING DEVELOPMENT OF SHARED LEADERSHIP

Shared leadership is not an alternative to hierarchical leadership: They go hand in glove. Without ongoing support and maintenance from hierarchical leadership, shared leadership is likely to be far less-than-optimal. Thus, here we describe how hierarchical leaders can encourage the ongoing development of shared leadership in organizations. First and foremost, it is critical to recognize that as a hierarchical leader you are a role model, whether you want to be or not. Thus, as a formal leader you must both talk-the-talk and walk-the-walk. For example, in a recent study we found that the best predictor of how subordinates engage in leadership is how their immediate supervisors' engage in leadership. This means that if you want petty dictators below you, simply act like one yourself. But if you want shared leadership to thrive consider your actions very carefully. According to Dave Berkus, of Tech Coast Angels, for instance, "You have to constantly demonstrate trust and confidence in people if you want to unleash their leadership potential." As such, you might ask for, rather than propose, solutions; encourage initiative, goal setting, and problem solving; model productive conflict management; and demonstrate application of strategies for both engaging in influence as well as being a willing recipient of influence. At a minimum, if you take nothing else away from this book, we recommend that you begin frequently using the four most empowering words a leader can use: "What do you think?" (Figure I.2).

Although shared leadership has been strongly linked to many positive organizational outcomes, our research is also very clear that shared leadership works best in tandem with leadership from above. However, beyond the four behavioral approaches to leadership we discussed above there are a couple of specific things hierarchical leaders can do to help promote effective shared leadership.

For one thing, periodic hierarchical leader intervention is going to be required in order to keep an organization headed on the right course. According to Leslie E. Stocker of the Braille Institute of America, "Encouraging shared leadership does have some risk. For example, I recall a situation where some wanted us to become involved in a new initiative and secured the external funding to make it happen. However, to me the initiative represented 'mission drift,' and I had to try to refocus our volunteers on our mission. We lost at least one volunteer over that issue." Thus, another important role for you as the hierarchical leader is stepping in and clarifying the overarching vision and values for the organization. It is also important for hierarchical leaders to ensure expectations are clear, and that performance is evaluated accordingly. Of course, you also need to ensure that appropriate training in leadership skills is provided. Naturally, we explore

The Four Most Important
Words in Leadership

Figure I.2 What do you think?

these, and many other topics in greater depth throughout the various chapters of this book.

SUMMING IT UP

Taken together, the organizations reported in this book represent a wide variety of contexts spanning from the not-for-profit world to high growth entrepreneurial firms to well established global organizations. What do these successful organizations all have in common? They have all developed their own unique recipe for sharing leadership. The rest of this book dives deeply into their stories. Our hope and intent is that you will pull the lessons that are most relevant to you from their examples and develop your own unique approach to tapping the human potential in your organization by sharing the lead.

SECTION I

ROTATED SHARED LEADERSHIP

This section focuses on rotated shared leadership. Shared leadership can be considered rotated when influence passes from one person to another (one at a time) in a planned purposeful way over time. In many ways, this can be considered the most basic form of shared leadership. That said; we do not wish to downplay the importance of rotated shared leadership. To the contrary, shared leadership comes in many forms and it needs to be tailored to organizational circumstances. The two primary examples of rotated shared leadership in this section are, Alcoholics Anonymous and the University of Maryland Trauma Center. Both demonstrate how a purposeful strategy of rotating shared leadership is an incredibly powerful development tool. We hope you can draw some useful lessons from their examples to apply to your organizations.

CHAPTER 1

ALCOHOLICS ANONYMOUS PAVES THE ROAD TO RECOVERY WITH SHARED LEADERSHIP

Zac Henson, Craig L. Pearce, and Charles C. Manz

Our leaders are but trusted servants; they do not govern
—Alcoholics Anonymous

FUNDAMENTAL CHAPTER THEME

Establish a shared focus among all stakeholders (both organization members and clients) on a higher purpose that transcends the people involved.

One of the more fascinating organizations that consciously deploys rotated shared leadership—an organization that is hyper-altruistic, if we can use that term—is Alcoholics Anonymous. Alcoholics Anonymous is founded on the very principles of shared leadership. To whet your appetite, so to speak, following are several excerpts from the Twelve Traditions—not to be confused with the Twelve Steps—of Alcoholics Anonymous: "Our

---

Share, Don't Take the Lead, pages 3–14

common welfare should come first; personal recovery depends upon A.A. unity...Our leaders are but trusted servants; they do not govern...Each group should be autonomous except in matters affecting other groups or A.A. as a whole...Every A.A. group ought to be fully self-supporting, declining outside contributions...Alcoholics Anonymous should remain forever non-professional." Alcoholics Anonymous has no designated leaders; there is no hierarchy: They are self-governing and practice an extreme form—perhaps the most extreme form—of shared leadership. See Boxes 1.1 and 1.2 for a full listing of the 12 Steps and 12 Traditions.

BOX 1.1—THE TWELVE STEPS

1. We admitted we were powerless over alcohol—that our lives had become unmanageable.
2. Came to believe that a power greater than ourselves could restore us to sanity.
3. Made a decision to turn our will and our lives over to the care of God as we understood Him.
4. Made a searching and fearless moral inventory of ourselves.
5. Admitted to God, to ourselves, and to another human being the exact nature of our wrongs.
6. Were entirely ready to have God remove all these defects of character.
7. Humbly asked Him to remove our shortcomings.
8. Made a list of all persons we had harmed, and became willing to make amends to them all.
9. Made direct amends to such people wherever possible, except when to do so would injure them or others.
10. Continued to take personal inventory and when we were wrong, promptly admitted it.
11. Sought though prayer and meditation to improve our conscious contact with God as we understood Him, praying only for knowledge of His will for us and the power to carry that out.
12. Having had a spiritual awakening as the result of these steps, we tried to carry this message to alcoholics and to practice these principles in all our affairs.

BOX 1.2—THE TWELVE TRADITIONS

1. Our common welfare should come first; personal recovery depends upon A.A. unity.
2. For our group purpose there is but one ultimate authority—a

loving God as He may express Himself in our group conscience. Our leaders are but trusted servants; they do not govern.
3. The only requirement for A.A. membership is a desire to stop drinking.
4. Each group should be autonomous except in matters affecting other groups or A.A. as a whole.
5. Each group has but one primary purpose—to carry its message to the alcoholic who still suffers.
6. An A.A. group ought never endorse, finance or lend the A.A. name to any related facility or outside enterprise, lest problems of money, property and prestige divert us from our primary purpose.
7. Every A.A. group ought to be fully self-supporting, declining outside contributions.
8. Alcoholics Anonymous should remain forever non-professional, but our service centers may employ special workers.
9. A.A., as such, ought never to be organized; but we may create service boards or committees directly responsible to those they serve.
10. Alcoholics Anonymous has no opinion on outside issues; hence the A.A. name ought never to be drawn into public controversy.
11. Our public relations policy is based on attraction rather than promotion; we need always maintain personal anonymity at the level of press, radio and films.
12. Anonymity is the spiritual foundation of all our traditions, ever reminding us to place principles before personalities.

ALCOHOLICS ANONYMOUS PAVES THE ROAD TO SELF-LED RECOVERY WITH SHARED LEADERSHIP

Alcoholics Anonymous (AA) provides fertile ground for leadership to emerge from the most unexpected sources. Compassion-oriented organizations like AA, that serve clients with acute levels of need and suffering (e.g., addiction, hunger, disease) that are resistant to sustainable solutions, face daunting challenges. Often treatment needs to be adjusted to adapt to the specific needs of individual clients. In addition, some who are suffering may be incapacitated, in denial, or feel too embarrassed to actively seek support and thus must be reached out to by others who can help. This makes the very clients being served, who have, for example, experienced the powerful and insidious nature of alcohol addiction, uniquely qualified to lead other clients with empathy and informed care. In fact, at AA, clients who have experience with the struggles involved and have a deep commitment to meeting the challenges of alcoholism, serve as pivotal leaders for other clients in an overall system of shared leadership.

Below we examine the specific case of Charlie Redhawk. AA develops leaders though a self-led process of servanthood fostered by shared leadership. This phenomenon occurs when the group dynamic transforms and adapts to culture, geography and language of members who support one another. Often, unlikely candidates (client members) in a group setting (AA Meetings) become leaders of a specific meeting via an unstructured shared leadership process. Like Charlie Redhawk, these leaders-of-the-moment, help establish a shared focus on a higher purpose—to break free from alcohol addiction through mutual support and leadership of one another—beyond any particular persons present (or not present) at the meetings.

THE UMATILLA INDIAN TRIBE AND CHARLIE REDHAWK: AN UNLIKELY SHARED LEADERSHIP CHAMPION

This story begins in 1994 in Pendleton, Oregon home of the Umatilla Indian Tribe. The Umatilla tribe consists of approximately 2,000 members of whom 600 reside on the reservation. In the tribe there are two distinct groups:

1. Those members who possess a self-led drive and a conviction for aspiring to greater heights of social position
2. Those who are satisfied with a passive subsistence of government provided cheese and locally killed Elk meat.

Most members who aspire to greater opportunities leave the reservation for urban lifestyles. Those who choose the reservation lifestyle have a strong propensity to lack the self confidence and initiative needed for self-leadership in their lives. Consequently, many fall victim to many social ills including alcohol, drug abuse, and dysfunctional family behaviors. Spousal abuse, for example, is a symptom of the chronic drug and alcohol abuse and it is a common part of the reservation crime scene according to the reservation police.

The power of the program of Alcoholics Anonymous is founded on in-group meetings, self-evaluation and personal inventory of character defects, and to perform a spiritual and psychological process described as "working the steps". This is a 12-step program that includes a self-appraisal, confession, repentance, and restitution. Miraculous transformations occur as a result of this program and involve individuals previously diagnosed as untreatable by the medical community. This is the backdrop from which Charlie Redhawk emerged as the unlikely leader. His clinical diagnosis was Wernicke-Korsakoff syndrome, commonly known as "wet brain". Despite his handicap he kept alive a weekly meeting *without any attendance* by other members for more than two years. That's right. . . . he was the only person at these meetings. So what would motivate such a self-sacrificing commitment, from an individual that suffered a condition of partial brain paralysis?

When asked this question he answered, "It keeps me sober". The self-leadership that he demonstrated was, ultimately, the inspiration for fellow tribal members to take on their own addictions and break free via the AA process.

A major casino construction project occurred that same year which required workers to be hired from the reservation's labor pool. The construction project used the AA meeting venue as a labor hall to solicit workers because of the human qualities sobriety provided. We found they all shared a common thread, which was a desire to stop drinking. In fact, that is the only requirement for membership according to the traditions adopted by the AA membership.

AA meetings typically last approximately one hour and after a meeting concludes there is some brief continued personal interaction. Many bonds and friendships are borne out of the meetings and a form of mentoring is encouraged which in AA terms is described as "sponsorship."Although not formally recognized in the writings or teachings, these relationships constitute a one-on-one support network for developing the needed self-leadership of each member and the subsequent shared leadership it engenders.

This network supports accountability and a type of "kinship" that is forged between members like *survivors of a shipwreck*. From the one meager member "meeting" of Charlie Redhawk, emerged, during the next two years, a membership of between 25 and 30. At last account, there are now two meetings a week with similar attendance long after the passing of Charlie.

Three key themes emerged as central to shared leadership in these AA meetings: the use of storytelling, the importance of being a voluntary servant leader, and an emphasis on psychological safety.

STORIES: A KEY TO SHARED LEADERSHIP AT AA

The significance of storytelling is the connection that occurs when personal testimony resonates with others' personal experience on an emotional level. Logical experiential association and learning at the expense of others has little permanent effect unless followed, at once, with a searching and fearless moral inventory. In essence, the storytelling provides a mechanism to set egos aside; to emphasize that the members are peers, and this suspension of ego facilitates the sharing of leadership across the group as members empathize, understand, support, and influence one another. As such, the practices and norms that define influence relationships among members of the AA meeting are an excellent example of rotating shared leadership in action.

In AA, autobiographical stories are transformational in both their content and function, and serve as a primary form of leadership influence. The storytelling in AA does not have a tightly prescribed structure but members are encouraged to share their personal experiences in a sequence of:

1. What was it like during your drinking career?
2. What happened to change your life (a critical incident, crisis, or point of disarray that AA members refer to as "hitting bottom")?
3. What is your new life like now, in the ongoing process of recovery?

Like many alcoholics' process of recovery, this narrative isn't necessarily linear—there are often ups and downs, relapses and returns to the program. However, even the relapses and daily challenges become opportunities to talk about one's good fortune for being present at the meeting and engaged in one's program of recovery.

In addition, AA members refer to alcoholism as a "disease" that creates insanity in the alcoholic. The temporary reprieve from this insanity can be practiced in the first of the 12 steps: "admitting you are powerless over alcohol and your life has become unmanageable." This insanity could be characterized as a seemingly hopeless state of mind and body. An untreated Alcoholic will drink even though he or she is clearly cognizant that the consequences of such an action will have severe detrimental effects. This anesthetic from the discomfort of abstinence brings a great remorse, yet the Alcoholic, despite such consequences, will repeat this behavior frequently. This is the very definition of insanity.

This becomes the essence of "one day at a time, one hour at a time, one minute at a time," a commonly prescribed practice at AA meetings. This restoration to sanity is further described as a spiritual footing in AA's third step: "We came to believe that a power greater than ourselves could restore us to sanity." The premise is that the natural state of consciousness is that of periodic insanity brought about by many factors. The alcoholic self-medicates this insanity absent the tools prescribed by AA.

The stories are also transformational in their effect on fellow AA participants through the modeling of "experience, strength, and hope," by AA participants who have made it through the recovery process to a point of "sanity" in their lives. Role models may be found in any member of the group, and are not limited to members who have flawless track records in their process. Also, longevity, seniority, and attendance alone do not appear sufficient to ensure recognition as a leader within the group.

Even members who go through a process of relapse and return can serve as models and reminders to others of their own process. Paradoxically, the role models' fallibility and struggles can simultaneously serve as an example while also maintaining a focus on the program itself and one's process of surrender to a higher power.

VOLUNTARY SERVANT LEADERSHIP

In AA's recovery program, autobiographical storytelling creates a collective process of connection and sense making. Another key part of AA's approach is founded on serving each other. Involving clients in serving and leading one another can help reduce costs of resource constrained compassion-oriented organizations such as AA. Further, these frequently non-profit firms can simultaneously benefit those they serve by tapping into the "built-in" empathy of past and current clients in the service of other clients while reducing the need for paid employee involvement. Voluntary servant-leadership supports the sharing process through members' individual experiences and storytelling that helps members to re-conceive of themselves through shared narrative. This enables clients sharing in the leadership process to change from self-destructive patterns to more constructive behaviors associated with being a servant to other individuals struggling with alcohol addiction.

In fact, one of AA's traditions specifically states, "Our leaders are but trusted servants". The self-effacement reflected in these last quotes ties in closely with the value placed in AA on servant leadership, in which one leads by giving back and serving others. This is embodied in the twelfth step: "Having had a spiritual awakening as the result of these steps, we tried to carry this message to alcoholics, and to practice these principles in our affairs." Virtually every meeting ends with a call for volunteers to serve in supporting other AA members or in helping to manage the organization. To be of service is of the utmost importance in the program of AA inasmuch as it requires one to get outside oneself. To abandon the selfish, self centered human nature and gain a greater altruistic lens. Clearly, the members of AA embrace this philosophy as they have collectively created a self sustaining cadre of voluntary servant leaders who gain no money, property, or prestige from extraordinary efforts they expend in their efforts to further the cause of AA. Rather they simply gain the knowledge that they are doing the right thing. Paradoxically, by giving to others, members are able to also maintain and advance their own recovery process. This is quite different from the standard medical model; having said that, we caught up with Kari Halko Weekes, a skilled mental health professional, who has built a psychology practice based on shared leadership principles. See Box 1.3 for her story.

BOX 1.3—SHARING LEADERSHIP FOR BETTER MENTAL HEALTH: PROFILING KARI HALKO-WEEKES

The stereotypic understanding of mental health therapy is heavily skewed toward the Freudian model where the therapist, through education and credentials, is the undisputed expert, who both diagnoses the patient's problems and prescribes corrective courses of action and is the authority figure that develops apprentice therapists. This model is firmly embedded in popular media portrayals of this persona and it is reinforced by the medical community. The reality, however, at least in high performing psychology practices is, if anything, the polar opposite.

Let's start with a look at the therapist-patient relationship. Recent research clearly demonstrates that when patients "own" their treatment they are far more likely to improve than when they are simply told what to do by an authoritarian therapist. To be most successful there must be a give-and-take, leader-follower model where both participants in the relationship explore and create the treatment process together.

Moving to the development of apprentice therapists, or what most states label interns, the situation is similar, however, the challenge is perhaps even more difficult due to restrictive governmental regulation. State regulations tightly control how licensed therapists are to oversee and assume responsibility for the actions of their interns. The regulations vigorously encourage therapist micro-management of interns, in a regimented, bureaucratic manner. However, some pioneering therapists have leapfrogged the bureaucratic hurdles to fully engage interns in the learning, emerging, growing dialogue that prepares them to truly serve their future clients in more meaningful ways. Kari Halko-Weekes is just such a therapist. According to her, "we all lead this practice together; it is the best way for the interns to learn; it is the best way for clients to benefit; and frankly it is best for me as the formal leader." Halko-Weekes has developed a very successful practice in southern California because not only is she skilled in understanding, relating, encouraging and developing her clients, but also because she has learned to leverage her personal capabilities through shared leadership practices with the interns she mentors. Says Halko-Weekes, "We truly strive to have a series of mentor-protégé relationships where we all learn from each other."

EMPHASIS ON PSYCHOLOGICAL SAFETY

The complementary practice to self-focused sharing is non-judgmental listening, another contributor to safety and trust in the group. This is particularly important in the sponsor/sponsee relationship as a central point of role modeling and leadership influence. Ideally, through the sponsors' sharing of their own experiences and non-judgmentally inquiring into the sponsees' process through the 12 steps of the program, sponsees are provided with an opportunity to hold themselves accountable to stay on track. The experience and learning of sponsors from their own AA journey thus serves sponsees in a variety of ways.

The second half of the name says it all. . . . Anonymous. Anonyminity is the spiritual foundation ever reminding the self leaders in AA to place principles before personalities. This was the cornerstone laid by the founders Bill Wilson and Dr. Bob Smith over 70 years ago. To maintain anonymity and not draw attention to themselves, AA members state their first name only. When reference is made to an individual in press, radio or film, it is first name and first letter of last name (i.e., Bill W. or Bob S.). Maintaining anonymity helps to create a climate of psychological safety to facilitate the personal recovery of the members.

One of the Twelve Traditions states," A.A., as such, ought to "never be organized". What are the implications of having an organization with millions of members that states it ought to never be organized? As AA has no need for rules, hierarchical structure, discipline codes, or any traditional organizational systems, the members have more freedom. Here again, freedom provides another basis for ensuring psychological safety. Furthermore, its leaders are but trusted servants, they do not govern. The only requirement for AA membership is a *desire* to stop drinking. This creates an environment where there are no expectations for achievements. New members are welcomed by loving and caring people who have experienced similar fears.

AA is often referred to as the hospital for the soul. AA is a safe place to tell your story without fear of repercussions. Where, whoever you are and whatever you have done, you are accepted into the fellowship.

THE STORY OF MARK AND HIS SELF-LED
RECOVERY JOURNEY

This is the case of Mark who, by appearance, had the world in his corner and prosperity as only one dreams of. With that in mind, it is said that the only thing worse for an alcoholic than bad fortune, is good fortune. That was the case with Mark. He was the president of a division of a large construction conglomerate, six-figure salary, luxurious house, lovely wife, and three teenage children. The outward appearance to friends and neighbors was that of a family man, successful in his career, president of industry associations and invitations to all the prestigious social events.

Then, a sleepy Sunday morning on March 21, at around 8:30 am, I, the first author, received a phone call from Mark that he was in trouble. I asked what the trouble was and he said he had just been released from County Jail where he spent the night on a drunk driving charge. I asked what happened and he explained that last night he got drunk at a social function. Driving home, he overshot his driveway and drilled the neighbor's motorhome. The motor home fortunately had no occupants but he did manage to strike the car into the rear propane storage cylinder, which proceeded to explode and caused the motor home to ignite into a blaze. Very soon the police and fire first responders showed up at the scene and as neighbors watched in astonishment (and his wife and kids watched in terror) the handcuffs went on and off Mark went to jail.

Mark's life went from the penthouse to the outhouse in a matter of minutes. He asked me what to do. I asked, "Do you think you may have a problem with alcohol?" His reply was, "I'm not sure but right now I'm in a lot of trouble and I don't know what to do. You have encountered similar stuff and seem to be fine now, how did you do it?"

At this moment I was tempted to tell him about what to do, how to find a counselor, treatment center, and check in but a voice told me he has already heard all that. Instead, I shared a similar experience I had where after being out drinking until early morning hours I was interrogated by my wife. I took my pants off she discovered my underwear were on backwards. She asked if I had been drinking and with another woman and of course I denied all wrongdoing. She didn't buy it. Soon, I found my bags packed and on the front doorstep with a note that I needed to leave. She took the kids to her Mother's house. When I was gone she returned. I realized unless I got help and demonstrated a sincere desire to stop drinking, it was over.

Mark chuckled a little and then asked to meet. I agreed, and we met at the coffee house to share experiences. I suggested if he wanted the next day I would take him to a meeting of AA that I knew was in the area, and that he might get something out of it. He was reluctant at first, but I could see his mind weighing the options and he hesitatingly agreed. He could tell I had something he wanted but couldn't put his finger on it. . . . a kind of quiet inner peace and the ability to handle situations that customarily baffled him.

This is a demonstration of a program of attraction rather than promotion as described in AA. Mark admitted that his life had become unmanageable. The first step in recovery is to fully concede to your innermost self that your life has become unmanageable. The behaviors that are so self-destructive gain some sense of normalcy. Drinking, drugs, and infidelity become normal behavior and abstinence becomes uncomfortable. Mark took my suggestion and entered a treatment center in hopes of successful treatment of his chronic condition.

During his stay I visited him often and I could see the transformation in his personality occurring. He had more peace and comfort inside his own skin. This is something that I felt occur as I practiced the actions of getting outside of my self-centered behaviors and into servanthood. The notion that by helping others you are helping yourself was as foreign to me as it was to Mark when I began my journey.

Mark and I watched the behavior of his fellow patients in the group home either embrace the principles and move ahead in their lives, or reject them only to leave the program and head for the streets. The majority of people who enter the 30-day program never make it 30 days. I asked Phil Mangen, a treatment counselor what percentage stay for the full 30 days and how many leave prior to completion. He told me about 20% stay and of that about 20% stay sober for one year. I was taken aback with his answer.

I asked him how disheartening it must be to see how few effect the change in their lives that this transformational process provides. He said he is inspired by those who gain enough self-leadership from the sharing supportive AA process to make a difference in their lives. Fortunately, so far, Mark is one of the members who is successfully leading himself back to a healthy and fulfilling life.

Indeed, AA is a remarkable organization that incorporates powerful shared leadership that many of its members develop the self-leadership to stand on their own two feet and successfully face life's most difficult challenges.

CONCLUSION

AA puts the belief that one unifying power, determined by the individual's belief system, when conceded, commands the actions and attitudes to relinquish control over an individual's life. The notion that self-will and will power be substituted by a power greater than oneself is the core of the program. This power is defined as merely a power greater than oneself. The effectiveness of the group relies on the herd instinct. Leaders emerge and exchange roles in a free flowing environment during frequently held meetings. The story telling resonates to the listener through similarities in ones self-experience. These personal testimonies are the touchstone of a connection between the emotions of suffering, and what is described as recovery.

Recovery is defined as a release from a seemingly hopeless state of mind and body. This connection is so powerful it brings forth a change in the way life is viewed, and so transformed; a type of peace befalls the individual. This connection, or conversion, can be described as a "spiritual experience". The resulting change in behavior provides hope to the group. If these good things are happening to him, perhaps they can also happen for me. This personality metamorphosizes and changes angry, confused, and tormented people into those that show happiness, kindness, compassion, caring and understanding which attracts fellow group members. The group gatherings and membership is the fellowship of AA.

The program is articulated in the basic text and further defined in the 12 steps. The steps are meant to be suggestive and possess certain truths that when applied to life's behavior, result in the happy, hopeful, functioning members of AA's huge society. These transformed members, are the lighthouses that guide the troubled to safe harbors. This freedom from the bondage of oneself is found in the leadership of this leaderless society.

One of the group's traditions describes the principle of attraction, rather than promotion. No matter how hard the spouse tries, the business colleagues try, the family pressures, health and wealth concerns, incarceration and the gates of insanity or death, until such time that an individual concedes to his innermost self that there is a problem that cannot be overcome by sheer willpower, there is no chance for recovery.

The "secret sauce" of AA is using Shared Leadership processes to create effective self-leaders. Building on the 12 traditions, the groups use storytelling as a means of setting egos aside. By setting egos aside they can create favorable conditions for dynamic give and take between leadership and followership. Next, through the practice of voluntary servant leadership, effective role modeling demonstrates the path to recover effective self-leadership. Finally, by creating a safe environment AA enables honest open communication and learning, which facilitates the creation effective self-leadership and so the cycle continues as these effective self-leaders give back and share the lead.

CHAPTER TAKEAWAYS

1. A key to the success and sustainability as an organization of Alcoholics Anonymous (AA) is an emphasis on common values and ethics—together, they generate trust and strengthen the relationships among the leadership team and all stakeholders (including clients) throughout the organization.
2. Use communication between members to help the organization's mission and vision to be actualized. At AA, this is promoted not only at the leadership level but also throughout the organization, including among the clients who voluntarily serve one another.
3. Comprise the leadership of individuals with complementary skill sets. This combining of distinct and complementary leadership skills has enabled AA to handle the variety of challenges it has faced as an organization.
4. At AA, egos and personal agendas are held in check with self-discipline and wisdom. This focus "beyond-oneself" can help shared leadership to thrive via mutual caring and support.

CHAPTER 2

UNIVERSITY OF MARYLAND SHOCK TRAUMA CENTER ROTATES SHARED LEADERSHIP IN CRISIS SITUATIONS, DEPENDING ON SKILL LEVEL AND CRISIS SEVERITY[1]

Henry P. Sims, Jr., Samer Faraj, Seokhwa Yun, and Craig L. Pearce

So if it's an experienced doctor I can trust, I do very little in terms of intervening . . . if it is a more junior person, he might need a lot more guidance, so I often may end up actually doing more of the interviewing of the patient or examining the patient and directing the case

—Attending Surgeon

FUNDAMENTAL CHAPTER THEME

Rotate shared leadership depending on the skills of the people involved and the demands of the task at hand.

Share, Don't Take the Lead, pages 15–27
Copyright © 2014 by Information Age Publishing
All rights of reproduction in any form reserved.

What makes for effective leadership? We've all heard that same old question a hundred times. And, we've all heard the same answer: It depends. Naturally, all of us want to know how we should behave as a leader. What if, for example, you are an attending surgeon at a medical shock trauma center, how should you lead the trauma center teams that treat the patients that are brought to the center for emergency care? After all, lives are at stake. Therefore, should you share leadership or not? Below we address how this and other questions surrounding leadership are addressed in just such a situation.

This is a story about rotated shared leadership at the University of Maryland Shock Trauma Center. More specifically, this chapter deals with shared leadership in trauma teams that treat incoming patients. We mainly focus on empowering leadership from a hierarchical leader, which helps to create shared leadership from below. In fact, the principal means through which shared leadership is implemented in an organization is empowering leadership. In many ways, it is difficult to effectively implement shared leadership without empowering leadership from above. In this chapter, we describe the conditions under which trauma team leaders choose to use empowering leadership to create rotated shared leadership versus directive leadership, where they drive the activities and actions of the team members. Further, we describe how leadership is rotated and shared among team members and the contextual circumstances where shared leadership is more likely to be useful. Throughout the chapter, we use real-life stories and quotations taken from the trauma team members at the University of Maryland Shock Trauma Center. While the focus of this chapter is on emergency medical situations there are other types of medical practice—or other organizational settings, for that matter—that benefit from the engagement of shared leadership. See Box 2.1 for how shared leadership is deployed at Madonna Rehabilitation Hospital, for example.

BOX 2.1— ENGAGING THE WHOLE PERSON WITH SHARED LEADERSHIP AT MADONNA REHABILITATION HOSPITAL

Madonna Rehabilitation Hospital is a special place. Unlike most hospitals they focus specifically on rehabilitation of patients with brain and spinal cord trauma. And they are recognized as a world-wide leader in the field. How do they achieve such status?

According to Marsha Lommel, CEO of Madonna, there are two primary driving forces of their success. First, she stated, "We are a mission driven organization; we want to improve peoples' lives." Research clearly shows us that rallying around a common cause binds people together and helps to bridge the gaps in roles and responsibilities by helping people see more sharply how to contribute to the overarching purpose.

Second Lommel stated, "We trust and empower our people." But spend a little time at Madonna and it becomes clear that it is not just about trust and empowerment—it is also about giving people the tools they need to be successfully empowered: At Madonna, they place a premium on training and development. In fact, all new employees receive considerable leadership and teamwork training and development. Says Mark Hakel, Director of Education and Staff Development, support for such training and development runs throughout the organization. To wit, the CEO is personally involved in the onboarding process for nearly every single new hire.

The combination of their united mission and their commitment to training and development has resulted in an entire culture based on shared leadership principles. And the evidence bears this out: Their workforce ranks as one of the most highly engaged employees in the world, as measured by the Gallup survey of employee engagement. All of this translates into a place where people derive meaning work and produce superior results. Madonna Rehabilitation Hospital is truly a place to be admired.

THE SHOCK TRAUMA CENTER

The R. Adams Cowley Shock Trauma Center at the University of Maryland is a world renowned trauma center located in Baltimore, Maryland. It was the first dedicated trauma center in the United States and has pioneered many of the key practices in trauma medicine. "Shock trauma," as the center is known among physicians and in the state of Maryland, is self-contained in a six-story building that is physically co-located next to the larger general hospital and medical school. Out of the 458 trauma centers in the United States, only three have their own buildings. Since effective trauma care requires a patient to be stabilized within an hour of the trauma, time is of the essence. And, dedicated trauma facilities are designed so that all of the needed equipment is collocated for rapid access. The center operates a number of specialized subunits, including the 10-bay Trauma Resuscitation Unit (TRU), an Operating Room (OR) area with six separate rooms, a Post Anesthesia Care Unit (PACU), and an in-patient ward (82 beds). In addition, supporting functions such as x-rays, Computerized Axial Tomography (CAT) scans, a hyperbaric chamber, and clinical laboratories are all located in the same building. Most hospitals run trauma care as a service within the emergency department and do so by dedicating one or more beds for trauma and having a trauma team on call. At shock trauma, the scale of the operation is significantly larger, as it serves as the primary trauma care center for most of the state and for some cases brought in from nearby Washington, D.C. According to the state health agency, the center has approximately 6,000 admissions per year and is designated as the primary adult trauma center for the Baltimore metropolitan area of about 2,000,000 people. In addition, it serves severely injured or multi-system trauma patients statewide who may be stabilized first at a local trauma center before being transferred in from elsewhere.

Shock trauma is recognized worldwide as a leader in trauma care. The center treats patients who have received some injury, most often physical, caused by a disruptive action such as a fall, car accident, or gun shot. As a secondary purpose, the trauma center is a training and educational organization that prepares medical professionals, especially residents, for further professional practice. Due to the volume of patients who are seen there, a doctor who is training at the center can see one or two orders of magnitude the number of cases they would see elsewhere. Thus, doctors interested in trauma all but beg for the chance to train there. Every year, over 250 residents and fellows, scores of medical students, and hundreds of nurses, paramedics, and advanced practitioners train there. Shock trauma is staffed by approximately 250 specialists including surgeons, anesthesiologists, medical residents, nurses, specialty consultants, technicians, and associated support staff.

Life in a trauma center ranges from periods of pure boredom to intense crises. At any given moment, lives can be at stake. A patient comes to the center, typically by ambulance or helicopter, and sometimes is in danger of imminent death. Indeed, despite the best efforts of the team, some patients do die. The main effort of the trauma team is to "stabilize" the patient: That is, to make sure that the patient's respiration and other vital life systems are working. This treatment is called "resuscitation." Time in the center is precious: Trauma patients need to receive treatment within an hour from injury or their body goes into "shock" and their chances of survival are seriously reduced no matter the extent of medical treatment after that point.

The central organizational unit of the Trauma Center is the Trauma Resuscitation Team, which is cross-functional and interdisciplinary. The team is composed of several medical specialists, which include an attending surgeon, a fellow (an advanced resident in training to be an attending) an anesthesiologist, nurses, technicians (e.g., x-ray), surgery and trauma care residents (MDs training for a specialization), and medical students. The team is a short cycle intense task force.

Each patient is treated by a trauma team in a sequence of events that is urgent and interdependent. For example, while the surgeon performs primary and secondary surveys of the patient, the anesthesiologist examines the airway and administers medication, the nurse inserts an intravenous line and reports on vital signs, and technicians provide various supporting tasks, such as x-ray. Team composition is fluid; that is, members may come and go as needed, as multiple patients may be arriving and need immediate evaluation and treatment. Treatment is action oriented and under intense time pressure and the team typically interacts with the patient for a half hour to several hours. Moreover, leadership of the team is a highly salient issue in the center.

LEADERSHIP DURING TRAUMA RESUSCITATION

From a leadership viewpoint, the attending surgeon is the key figure on the team. The "attending," as this leader is called, is clearly in charge, and is in charge of the decision making in regard to the patient, as well as the task activities of the team members. The goals of the attending are

1. To ensure a successful resuscitation
2. To offer learning opportunities for team members, especially the residents—the MDs specializing in surgery.

These goals—to ensure an optimal outcome for the patient and to ensure learning—can sometimes be in conflict, and present a conundrum for the team leader. If one always optimizes 100% on patient safety, then most procedures would always be carried out by the attending surgeon who has the greatest skill and expertise. Yet, this would never provide an opportunity for the resident to develop new skills and knowledge. To wit, at some point, every resident must undertake a procedure for the very first time. From the leader's viewpoint, these conflicting goals provide a challenge of deciding when the resident should be empowered to share the lead regarding the care of a patient.

This issue is not unique to trauma teams. Other urgent situations, characterized by the need for rapid response and high reliability, such as air controller teams, nuclear power operator teams, or legal and consulting teams are examples of situations that present the same leadership challenge. When should I be directive? When should I empower and rotate the lead to those below?

Through the resuscitation, the attending surgeon is the formal and hierarchical leader, and can influence the team through various types of leadership. Even though team members may be highly trained in their own discipline, the attending has ultimate responsibility for the whole team's performance and the patient outcome. As one resident told us, "It is all on his credit card".

Accordingly, we often observed attending physicians engaging in directive leadership, where the leader personally determines the diagnosis, has "hands on" the patient, makes treatment decisions, and gives information and task direction to members of the team. Typically, this leadership is undertaken in a firm and urgent tone, yet it is occasionally obnoxious and aversive. This behavior is classic top-down leadership, with the attending surgeon clearly "taking charge" and assuming the role of centralized decision maker and task giver. A directive trauma team leader does not "share the lead," but instead, "takes the lead." Consider the following statement:

You see all kinds [of leadership]. Some of the doctors are very hands-on.... They immediately correct, if they see something wrong.... So, you can see things going on and you know this doctor is gonna react to that. [an observer in the trauma center]

We also found a second type of leadership to be common. This type clearly fitted the "empowering" approach we defined earlier, and is an example of rotating shared leadership to other team members. In this leadership mode, the attending surgeon delegated decision making to a resident, who then became the leader of the team for that particular patient.

So, what you really want to do is to get them just when they are getting ready to fall off the cliff and do something bad, and say you know, maybe you should give some thought to X. When the residents call me and tell me what do they want me to do with this patient, I say what I want you to do is to be a doctor. I want you to go stand by the patient, I want you to consider the possibilities, and I want you to tell me what you think and then we will discuss whether that is a good idea or bad idea [chief of surgery].

Empowerment of the resident develops over time. At first, the attending would require the resident to stand back and observe treatment of patients. Often, the attending would speak out loud, describing the situation, the decisions involved, and the rationale for undertaking a particular procedure. This verbal behavior is a form of direction and instruction.

At the next stage, the attending would ask the resident for recommendations. "Dr. Jones, what should we do now?" The attending would listen and give feedback to the resident about the correctness and appropriateness of the resident's recommendation, but would still perform the hands on procedures. In the third stage, the resident would perform the procedures, with the attending standing at the resident's shoulder, monitoring each decision and each task, providing direction and feedback only if necessary. In the fourth stage, the resident would have relatively full responsibility, with the attending surgeon standing back at the edge of the treatment bay, but still observing, and then later, providing post hoc critique and feedback. At the final stage, the resident would be given full responsibility, while the attending surgeon would still be available on the premises, but perhaps in another part of the Trauma Center. This last stage could be described as relatively full empowerment. Further, this "staging" or gradual development of the resident is a demonstration of how shared leadership can increase over time.

WHEN SHOULD LEADERSHIP BE SHARED?

A Situational Approach at the Shock Trauma Center

Our observations led to the question of why a leader would sometimes be directive, and at other times empowering. We observed many instances of both directive and empowering leadership on the part of attending surgeons, and that the particular situation often determined whether the leader was directive or empowering. The first and most important situational factor was the severity of the patient's injury. Was the patient's injury critical, or less threatening? Was the patient near death? Consider the following observation from one of the trauma team members:

> ...It depends on how critical the patient is. If the patient doesn't seem to be critical, you will see the fellow and the attending kind of roll out of the picture and kind of backing off and allowing team members kind of to carry things on. But if it gets escalated and [the patient] gets more critical hypertension, you will tend to see attending and fellow at the bedside, probably more see the attending make all the calls. So I guess it varies... [how] critical resuscitations are... you kind of try, allow people to learn how to do things. [An attending surgeon]

Another attending anesthesiologist raises the safety versus learning trade-off even more directly:

> I try with young healthy patients to give [the residents] more latitude; with people who are sicker, I often warn them ahead of time that I'm going to have a very quick whistle on this one if you don't get it right away, I'm going to have someone else do it or I'm going to do it myself. By and large, the residents understand this.

We observed a clear pattern. The more the patient's condition approached criticality, the more the leader tended to be directive. The logic in this finding is that a more severe injury required the highest degree of expertise that was available, and, that expertise was to be found in the attending surgeon. Moreover, time seemed to be a factor. Severely injured patients imposed more stringent time constraints. In contrast, when the injury was less severe, attending surgeons were much more willing to delegate decision making, hands on treatment, and to share leadership with the resident.

We found another situational characteristic to be an important factor in determining the surgeon's leadership was the degree of experience and expertise of the resident. Residents go through a time honored cycle in terms of the calendar and their learning curve. Typically, residents begin their one-year program on July 1. For the first month or two, their expertise is minimal, and also, typically, they are not empowered to any significant degree. But, as time goes by, the residents work hard and are exposed to a wide variety of patients, injuries, and conditions. They observe and receive instructions from the attending surgeons, and are generally eager to undertake decision making and procedures on their own. By the time several months have gone by their expertise has improved considerably and the attending surgeons become increasingly more willing to empower the residents. When June arrives, residents are typically fully empowered except under unusual circumstances. The main observation was that empowering leadership was critical in facilitating learning opportunities for the residents.

These two situational factors were not equally important in terms of their impact. The severity of patient injury seemed to be more dominant. That is, while both situational factors were significant, the attending surgeons tended to emphasize severity of patient injury as the more important situational factor. Even for a long-term medical observer [charge nurse], the specifics of the situation are the drivers:

> It depends on . . . who you are working with and what you need to get done. It just depends on, it depends on how sick the patient is, what you need to get done with the patient, how strong or weak the team is . . .

In summary, we uncovered a contingency practice of leadership that seemed to be specific to the unique environment of the Shock Trauma Center. When patient injury is severe and resident experience is low, attending surgeons are more likely to exercise directive leadership. When patient injury is less severe, and, when resident experience is high, attending surgeons are more likely to exercise empowering leadership and rotate the leadership to the appropriate resident-in-progress. This logic is represented by a decision diagram, shown in Figure 2.1. Also, this figure represents a "contingency view" or, a "situational model" where the use of rotated shared leadership depends on situational characteristics and the knowledge, skills and abilities of the individuals involved.

ISSUES SURROUNDING ROTATED SHARED LEADERSHIP

The trauma center receives a large range of trauma injuries including penetration wounds (e.g., a gunshot or knife wound), injuries from car crashes and falls, and patients requiring hyperbaric oxygen therapy (e.g., diving accidents, carbon monoxide poisoning). The workload varies significantly all day long and is impossible to predict. The trauma center has to plan for unexpected peaks in demand such as when a multiple motor vehicle crash or an industrial accident occurs. Bar closing times, rain and traffic rush

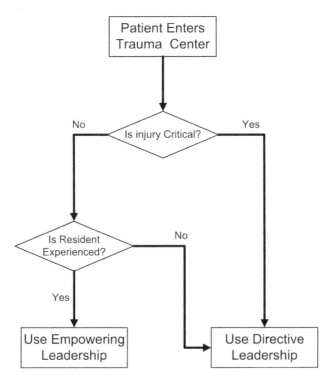

Figure 2.1 Simplified decision tree of how an attending surgeon selects a leadership style.

hours all affect the workload. The summer months are also busier as the higher temperatures allow people to engage in more outdoor activities. As the medical director points out, there is little control over what admissions come to the STC.

> This is a shock trauma center, so the only thing you can be sure of is that it's not going to happen the way that you expect it to happen. We do emergencies—that's what we do for a living. Several nights ago, we admitted 35 patients, 24 of them after 7 pm. We came within one of a shock trauma record, which I currently hold at 36 admissions in a day. At four am, we had 13–14 patients, and some people double bunked in the TRU. Then the city called and said that there was a house fire in the neighborhood and they were bringing us 4 patients, 3 of them had a cardiac arrest, and they will be there in 2 minutes.

Because incoming patients differ in their injury type and severity, the level of uncertainty that the trauma staff experiences is extremely high. Each patient is different and the treatment cannot be pre-specified and must be customized. Patients in critical condition are brought in with just minimal warning and treatment must begin promptly.

The treatment process requires an immediate assessment that leads to establishing a diagnosis that in turn leads to the selection of an appropriate treatment plan. Complications abound: Patients are often unconscious or disoriented and thus unable to provide information about medical history or allergies. By working against the clock and with limited information, the trauma team may too quickly establish a diagnosis and sometimes misses complications such as internal bleeding, allergy or a previous injury/illness that may impair the evolving treatment. Finally, the team is also generally working on several patients at the same time. The treatment process demands finely tuned interactions among nurses, surgeons, and anesthesiologists. The work requires complex forms of coordination. For example, the patient needs to be anesthetized before the surgeon can perform a surgical intervention. But the patient may react unexpectedly to surgery and thus require more frequent interventions by the anesthesiologist. Simultaneously, the team has to treat all admitted patients and is unable to focus on one patient at a time. Thus, these treatment complications combined with distributed expertise create unique challenges in leading such teams. Widely spread expertise works best when there is a strong reliance on shared leadership from the actors involved.

In order to safeguard patients, attending doctors (e.g., surgery) rely on flexible supervision rules of thumb and a healthy skepticism of the residents training under them; the collegial atmosphere and bantering covers up a well-developed authority structure. The attending surgeon (usually a professor) is the ultimate authority. Because the attending physician is often treating multiple patients in and out of the trauma center, a well developed leadership heuristic guides the team. If the attending is absent, the fellow (a resident doing advanced training) is in charge. If the fellow is also absent, seniority (as a proxy for expertise) defines leadership roles among residents. This leads to a responsibility system where each person leads those more junior. For example, a mistake made by a resident when the fellow is present is taken as a failure of the fellow. If the fellow is not present, the most senior resident is in charge and responsible. In that way, leadership is rotated and shared in an orderly fashion based on skills of the people at hand and provides the team with significant operational flexibility as the teams have to sometimes split to simultaneously treat more than one trauma victim. Note that seniority is a sort of surrogate for expertise; that is, more seniority adds up to more experience and greater expertise. It is risky to allow a newcomer to perform a procedure when there is no objective way to assess actual expertise. As an attending surgeon described how training and control are tightly intertwined:

So if it's an experienced doctor that I can trust, I do very little in terms of intervening, he can just do everything himself, I just will stand back and make sure everything is appropriate. If it is a more junior person, he might need a lot more guidance, so I often may end up actually doing more of the interviewing of the patient or examining the patient and directing the care of the patient...because this inexperienced doctor would not have done the correct things at the correct time. So depending on the skill level or the training level of that primary doctor, I need to be more or less involved in that patient.

An attending anesthesiologist confirms the point by describing his own heuristics:

Until I have seen them, I have a sort a 'rule of thumb;' that is we have to see 5 elective tracheal intubations in the operating room in a very controlled environment before we would consider, before we would let anyone, do any emergency intubations in the admitting area, because the admitting area is so much more stressful and so much more critical than an elective intubation in a well controlled environment.

In trauma care, leadership is naturally rotated among specialties due to the highly specialized expertise required. Medical interventions are organized by discipline. As an attending anesthesiologist exclaimed, "The responsibility of the airway is the anesthesiology team; responsibility of the belly issue is the surgical team." These interactions can, however, become touchy as opinions (i.e., medical judgments) differ as to how best to treat the patient. On occasion, the disciplinary focus leads to disagreements as to the next steps in treating the patient. Issues of work interdependence are present: A surgeon cannot perform surgery before the anesthesiologist anesthetizes the patient. The surgeon is often in a hurry to "get in there" and treat the injury. On the other hand, the anesthesiologist has to be cognizant of the overall state of the patient's health and the danger posed by putting a severely injured patient too quickly under anesthesia. This leads to differences of opinion. As an attending surgeon recognized:

You'll have that in terms of interdisciplinary issues. Typical case is I'm the attending trauma surgeon and there's an attending anesthesiologist, I think the patient should be intubated and the anesthesiologist doesn't. So who out ranks whom? Sometimes it goes by the level of seniority. Who has been there longer? Or it goes by who's more aggressive about standing firm, or the interpersonal relationship between the two.

Leadership is also rotated and shared with nurses in order to safeguard the all-important patient safety. Nurses, generally, have many more years of experience than the scalpel wielding residents in training. More importantly, the superordinate goals of the trauma center support the patient safety role of the nurses. As one technician described:

> If the resident is pushing for something that really seems outrageous to the nurse, that they'll say, "Well this is what you've asked us to do and this is what we're supposed to do and these are the consequences.

Thus, while nurses are technically subordinate, the mission critical nature of the situation gives them considerable power in the process of patient decision making.

In summary, shared leadership in trauma care is an important aspect of ensuring effective operations and the safety of the patient. As seen in the examples above, rotated shared leadership in practice generates interdisciplinary friction and may be difficult to accept for those doctors acculturated in the directive leadership style of medicine of old. However, the results achieved by the shock trauma center seem to indicate that a well managed approach to shared leadership can provide significant advantages in complex and dynamic work settings. So, the question for you is how should you determine how to rotate and share leadership in your organization?

CONCLUSION

Contingency or situational models of leadership deal with the notion that different circumstances call for different types of leadership. When should I use shared leadership? The general notion of situational adaptability to leadership certainly has intuitive appeal to anyone interested in leadership. Despite this challenge of situational adapting one's approach to leading from above, our findings from the Maryland Shock Trauma Center clearly show how rotating shared leadership can be situational in nature, and especially how shared leadership can be enhanced and developed over time.

In the shock trauma center, our investigation uncovered strong evidence that attending surgeons did, indeed, share their own leadership depending on the situation. We can speculate as to whether the results of our particular trauma center project might apply to other situations. The most straightforward linkage would be to organizational situations where emergency or crisis issues are salient—for example, fire fighting, natural disaster response, public safety; other situations where lives are at stake. Yet, we also believe that these issues are also present in non emergency, everyday organizational situations. In a software development team, for example, we would expect that the degree of empowerment would depend on how timely and critical the project due date, and the experience of members of the development team. Overall, we advocate that leaders be generally less prone to share leadership when subordinates are less experienced, and when the particular project or task is absolutely timing critical to the organization. We also advocate that leaders be more encouraging of shared leadership when they have a deliberate agenda to develop the skills and experiences of their followers.

One important contribution of this chapter was the discovery of a general approach to defining the specific situational elements within a particular environment, and developing guidelines of how leadership can be optimized within that environment. Each of us can approach the question of shared leadership from a perspective that is unique to our own situation. Indeed, there is an answer to whether leadership should be shared, and, not surprisingly, "it really does depend!"

CHAPTER TAKEAWAYS

1. Contrary to the popular belief that in a crisis situation you need strong centralized leadership, the University of Maryland Trauma Center clearly demonstrates that it is a combination of strong centralized and strong shared leadership that is the best at addressing crises.
2. In crisis situations, rotate leadership based on expertise. At the University of Maryland Trauma Center, knowledge needed to meet patient urgent needs frequently trumps hierarchical authority— experienced Nurses are relied upon more than an inexperienced Intern MD.
3. Adjust the leadership process based on situational requirements. The severity of patient needs and the experience level of the medical team members should determine the way leadership is rotated.

SECTION II

INTEGRATED SHARED LEADERSHIP

In this section we examine integrated shared leadership, which is a more advanced form of shared leadership, as the term suggests. Shared leadership can be considered integrated when influence is not just passed from person to person in a linear way but often unfolds as a simultaneous and reciprocal process of mutual influence. The organizations highlighted in this section include the serial entrepreneurs that launched both Palm Pilot and Handspring and Southwest Airlines. The serial entrepreneurs are super clear about how integrated shared leadership was critical to the success of their ventures. Meanwhile, Southwest, the only continuously profitable major U.S. airline, has long established itself as an outside the box innovative company that has succeeded in a struggling industry. They are a massive company, with nearly 40,000 employees, which they simply call co-workers. They encourage irreverence, individuality, and empowerment. They hire on attitude and train for skills. They are fascinating and show what is possible, even in an extremely large enterprise when one unleashes the potential of shared leadership. Their progressive leadership approach—which relies on shared leadership throughout the firm—is a prominent aspect of how they have set themselves apart for high performance in the face of difficult challenges confronting major airlines that have driven much of their competition into bankruptcy. There are some important lessons to be drawn from the examples highlighted in this section, which we hope you can apply in your own circumstances.

CHAPTER 3

FROM PALM PILOT TO SMARTPHONE WITH SHARED LEADERSHIP AS THE GLUE THAT BINDS SERIAL ENTREPRENEURS

Ronald M. Baglio, Jai Gupta, and Charles C. Manz

I can't ever recall a time managing our business where I found myself asking
"What is best for me?" versus "What is best for us?"

—Jeff Hawkins

FUNDAMENTAL CHAPTER THEME

Effectively combine complementary leadership skills for sustained entrepreneurial success.

Integrated shared leadership, as a management philosophy, allows for the distribution of responsibilities and decision-making so that an organization can maximize the usefulness of the employee base upon which the company

Share, Don't Take the Lead, pages 31–50
Copyright © 2014 by Information Age Publishing
All rights of reproduction in any form reserved.

is built. Drawing upon the human resources that a company has available enhances the likelihood of devising the best strategies, developing the most thoughtful design, or producing the most competitive product. To remain competitive, organizations can ill-afford to be narrowly defined in mission and vision. Shared leadership provides an opportunity for an organization to exhaust the possibilities to develop a well-informed and well-thought out corporate system.

One exciting and potent example of shared leadership in action takes place when a top management team works together, mutually influencing one another, to launch a new firm. Certainly, there are many challenges that face a newly formed company. Decisions about product development, business planning, corporate philosophy and mission are critical to the health and sustainability of an organization. And, arguably, the most critical part of this process has to do with the development of the company's leadership style from top to bottom.

At times, the style is dictated by the needs of the organization or the makeup of the staff. Other times, this style is dictated by the specific product that a company is developing or the line of work that the company engages in. Most often, the significant influence comes from the top leaders' styles and orientations, as they are largely responsible for creating the vision and the conditions for the birth and growth of the enterprise. While all of these factors need to be considered for the shared leadership model to be effective, here we give particular attention to complimentary skill sets among a company's leadership team and the resulting competitive edge.

The following chapter provides an inside look at the shared leadership process and activities of the team that brought us Palm, Inc. This remarkable team thrived on a shared leadership philosophy that revolutionized the computing world and produced two successful startup ventures, Palm Inc. and Handspring. The pooled talents and efforts of Ed Colligan, Donna Dubinsky, and Jeff Hawkins brought handheld computers and smartphones into the mainstream; landmark advances in personal electronics that would not have been possible without their shared leadership philosophy and approach within an entrepreneurial context.

Each of the shared leadership team offered their individual takes on the success they experienced as a team. Dubinsky begins, "The partnership with Jeff was essential to my being a successful entrepreneur. At Apple and Claris (Dubinsky's initial experiences in the technology field), I worked with other product leaders. I knew that I didn't have the skill set. In order to be a successful entrepreneur, I needed to find somebody who was great at designing products. The partnership with Ed was a little less critical [initially] in that it was more of an overlap with my skills. But as the company got bigger, his role became more and more essential. Ultimately, at Handspring, I could just leave sales and marketing to him, allowing me to focus in other areas, particularly finance, HR, IT, customer service, repair, and manufacturing."

Hawkins echoed that sentiment. "I always knew that I didn't want to run a business. When I received my first round of funding, I [knew that] eventually we would have to hire a CEO but I did not know what working with a CEO would be like. Often the founding entrepreneur has a falling out with the new management and leaves. What I learned after working with Donna and Ed was that a good partnership is the best structure. They helped me be successful and vice versa."

Colligan adds, "Always act with the highest integrity when working with your employees and partners. Work as one team—we're all in this together and in good times or bad it is a collective celebration or issue to solve."

Every step of the way, the leadership team approached critical decisions utilizing the specific skill sets of the individuals that comprised it. The marketing genius of Ed Colligan, the business savvy of Donna Dubinsky, and the technological ingenuity of Jeff Hawkins factored into every step the organization took as it grew from start-up to industry powerhouse. Their shared leadership model was critical in initiating successful processes and sustaining healthy practices. We will be discussing the team's model of leadership in more detail later in this chapter. First, however, we will provide a brief business history that includes some beginning details concerning the role leadership played in the evolution of this shared leadership team. (For a brief historical timeline for this chapter see Appendix 1).

PALM, INC.: A HANDS-ON APPROACH
TO HANDHELD TECHNOLOGY

The early 1990s were exciting times in the world of personal computing. As technology became more affordable and accessible to the general public, early visionaries of the personal computer industry looked to shrink technology, making the personal computer smaller and more portable. The innovators who shaped personal computing were interested in adapting their product in meaningful ways to meet the needs of a society that was not only on the move but moving at an ever-increasing pace. Jeff Hawkins was one such innovator.

An electrical engineer by training, Hawkins envisioned a device that literally brought the personal computer to the palm of your hand. To realize that dream, Palm Computing was founded in 1992. At this time, founder, Hawkins teamed with Chief Executive Officer, Donna Dubinsky and together they aggressively pursued their vision for the handheld computer market. While the early products may seem limited in application by today's standards, their ideas were revolutionary for the time and caught the eye and imagination of investors and industry leaders alike.

Their initial foray into business focused on software development. Dubinsky explains, "Our first software application was the PIM, personal information manager. This included a calendar, address book, memo pad and to-do list. Our first deal was to write the PIM for a Tandy handheld computer, the Zoomer. It was bundled with the software." Eventually, Palm developed connectivity software for existing portable devices. Primarily, this software enabled these narrowly applied devices, for example, writing tablets (hardware that digitized handwritten notes for electronic storage) and personal organizers (electronic calendars), to communicate with desktop personal computers.

The company began to grow, both literally and figuratively. Dubinsky and Hawkins were soon joined by marketing expert, Ed Colligan. Together, they pushed Palm toward an exciting future. In 1994, Palm created another stir in the industry with the advent of their new handwriting recognition software, Graffiti. Up to that point, people seeking to enter information into a portable device needed to do so by using an on-screen keyboard with a small plastic pointer. The process was tedious and often imprecise. The ability to write notes and enter information with a fluid process sped up data entry and made portable electronics a more attractive tool. At the same time, Hawkins and the design team of Palm were developing their own handheld computer. This remarkable innovation brought attention, notoriety, and yes, opportunity to Palm, ultimately resulting in its sale to US Robotics in 1995.

The influx of capital that came with the acquisition allowed Palm to introduce their signature product—the Palm Pilot —to the market in 1996. The Palm Pilot was a small, but brilliant, personal digital assistant (PDA) that allowed users to manage data and collect information while they were away from their office. It included the Graffiti handwriting recognition software and communication software that enabled the fast and easy exchange of information with the PC by simply placing the Palm Pilot into a cradle that plugged into the computer. In 18 months, more than 1,000,000 Palm Pilot s were sold. While the PDA market was establishing itself and many technology companies were jockeying for position, US Robotics (Palm's parent company) was purchased by 3Com in 1997 and more change was afoot for the Palm leadership team.

HANDSPRING: A NEW DIRECTION, AN OLD FORMULA

Despite good press about the Palm Pilot and the leadership team's success in bringing the device to market, it was clear that the challenges associated with the 3Com purchase would be daunting. The emotions and the politics involved were captured well in the *Forbes* magazine article, Three's Company:[1]

> 3Com was slow to recognize the Palm's increasingly vertical growth trajectory, focusing instead on integrating Palm into its global strategy . . . Hawkins remembers his own frustration: "We were working with one hand behind our backs. We wanted to develop new products and push in new directions. But we found ourselves only a division of 3Com, a big, slow-moving company." Dubinsky, supported by Hawkins and Colligan, pressed 3Com executives to spin Palm off. There were numerous deliberations, but the outcome was always the same: no dice. "Finally, after one last plea, I got up from the table and said, 'Okay, I'm going to have to resign,'" Dubinsky recalls, her ice blue eyes alight with the memory. "Then I walked into Jeff's office and told him the news." Recalls Hawkins, "She came in and said, 'You just quit.'"

As a result, in August of 1998, Dubinsky and Hawkins left Palm to form Handspring. Initially, Colligan remained with 3Com to see if he would be appointed CEO. After several months, it became obvious that this would not happen and he joined Handspring as well. Interestingly, the team had no specific plan or product in mind at that point. What they did have was a trust in each other and their mutual experience of the successful venture in establishing Palm as a force in the hi-tech industry. They also had a reputation in the field and the confidence to quickly begin work on the next big thing.

Each member of the team shared in the leadership process by taking the lead in their strength areas. Hawkins began working in earnest in his garage to develop the next generation of handhelds. Meanwhile, Dubinsky and Colligan went about the business of establishing a new company and securing financing for their next endeavor. Their individual efforts and combined team synergy led to success on all fronts. In September of 1999, the Handspring Visor was born.

The Visor distinguished itself from the Palm Pilot in that it had the ability to add on hardware, allowing it to morph itself into a much more complicated device without losing the portability of a handheld. The Visor was created with the capacity to become a pager, a digital camera or even a cell phone by plugging the associated hardware into what was referred to as the Springboard slot (an adapter slot). This revolutionary flexibility was yet another market-transforming nuance that resulted from the team's highly effective shared influence process.

From the standpoint of shared leadership, the complementary skills of each team member allowed the team to make effective decisions without stretching too far from his or her comfort zones. The diverse backgrounds and experiences provided the necessary pool of knowledge for the team to draw from. While there were certainly challenges, stressful times, and mistakes, the organization benefited from trust that its team members had in each other. The team used this trust to cement their commitment to consumer-focused handhelds, and ultimately to develop the next stage of mobile computing, the smartphone. Their first product, the Handspring Visor was a huge success. In its fifth quarter of existence, Handspring generated over 100 million dollars in revenue. Dubinsky puts this into perspective, "At our fifth or sixth quarter of doing business, I believe we were among the fastest growth companies in American history from inception. Our revenue was at a 400 million dollar run rate."

BACK TO THE BEGINNING: HANDSPRING IS PURCHASED BY PALM

Over the course of the next five years, the Handspring leadership team rode the highs and lows of the technology market. They faced many challenges along the way. The economics of the market notwithstanding, Handspring continued to gain momentum as the smartphone progressed through the developmental process. Combining the flexibility of the PDA with the communication network capability of cellular telephony, the Handspring Treo was the next significant breakthrough success of the shared leadership trio of Colligan, Dubinsky, and Hawkins. It marked yet another noteworthy accomplishment of the Colligan, Dubinsky, and Hawkins team's amazing ten year run.

At the same time, the original Palm experienced a significant transformation during the five years after the shared leadership team departed. Less than 14 months after 3Com refused to spin off Palm, fostering the leadership team's decision to launch Handspring, 3Com made an about face and spun off Palm after all, as the handheld leader continued to develop new products and software to support their family of PDAs. After experiencing the highs of stellar sales of subsequent versions of the successful Palm Pilot and the Palm Operating System, the reality of the bursting of the Internet bubble and the near recession of the American economy forced Palm to restructure and downsize. Despite the corresponding decline in performance, this defensive effort enabled Palm to survive the tightening technology market.

Simultaneously, Handspring was experiencing the squeeze of the economic downturn. The combination of market circumstances, production challenges, and some difficult management decisions created a need for change for Handspring as well ... ultimately leading our focal leadership team of Colligan, Dubinsky, and Hawkins "back to the future." In June of 2003, Palm announced the purchase of rival Handspring. Dubinsky explains, "From the strategy side, the two companies had evolved in complimentary directions. Palm had invested heavily in handheld computers, developing some nice products, while Handspring had pretty much stopped producing handhelds in favor of smartphones. The merger could yield a stronger company financially, with a broad product portfolio with little overlap."

While a challenge for all involved, the streamlining of both firms through corporate fusion allowed these organizations to survive. The Treo smartphone remained a market force and Palm remained a player in the mobile computing field.

In the acquisition, Colligan, Dubinsky, and Hawkins played different parts than they had in the past. Realizing that Palm was now a different beast from the organization they first founded in 1992, each of the team members took on new roles. Donna Dubinsky accepted a position on Palm's Board of Directors. (The Board oversees the direction and mission of the organization while leaving the day-to-day operation of the organization to the management team.) Jeff Hawkins assumed the position of Palm's Chief Technology Officer. Ed Colligan was eventually named Palm's Chief Executive Officer and he continued to play that role.

With the success of Palm and Handspring already cemented, Dubinsky and Hawkins showed no signs of stopping. In 2005, they undertook a new venture, Numenta, seeking to commercialize Hawkins' theory of neocortical operation as laid out in his book, "On Intelligence," (In layman's terms, Numenta seeks to develop software that allows computers to process information the same way the human brain works.). In his book, Hawkins acknowledged his reliance on Donna Dubinsky and Ed Colligan, and in so doing, reinforced the importance of shared leadership that took place among the entrepreneurs. He writes: "Through their hard work and assistance, I was able to be an entrepreneur while simultaneously working part-time on brain theory, an unusual arrangement... This book wouldn't exist if it weren't for Donna and Ed."[2]

CHALLENGES FOR THE SHARED LEADERSHIP OF PALM

There are times when leaders choose the style they wish to cultivate in their workplaces and then there are times when the leadership style is dictated by the specific assets and deficits in the skill sets of the leadership team. For the founders of Palm, the latter was definitely the case. Donna Dubinsky was a business person with a sense of purpose and the traditional leadership skills necessary to handle all of the intricacies of the day-to-day operations. Jeff Hawkins was an inventor and relatively unconcerned with the leadership demands of running an organization. Ed Colligan was a marketing wizard. Originally, the three did not look to establish a partnership as they forged their personal careers. Eventually, the partnership evolved. And while the partnership may have been fruitful, the road was not without hazards.

The leadership team faced many challenges as they established themselves both within their organization and within the business world at large. In many ways, these challenges threatened the viability of a shared leadership model. Yet the successful negotiation of these challenges solidified the utility of shared leadership for Palm, and for the three leaders who brought it to life.

EGOS, EXPECTATIONS, AND BALANCE

It would be naïve to view Palm's three person leadership team as an easy puzzle in which all of the pieces fell neatly into place. Each of the individuals came to the venture with varying experiences and differing opinions on how to successfully run a company. Each had unique individual strengths and experiences that together enabled them to practice shared leadership in a synergistic and particularly fruitful way. While Jeff Hawkins may be characterized as a scientist holed up in his garage trying to save the world with his ingenious inventions, Hawkins is also a brilliant individual who had a vision of how he wanted the inventions to be developed, marketed, and sold. While it was out of his area of expertise, he was still passionate about the business side of this process.

Similarly, Donna Dubinsky had aspirations. At the time that she first encountered Jeff Hawkins, she was actively looking for an opportunity to be a CEO. She had established herself as CEO material by demonstrating business savvy in traditional business settings. While she clearly recognized the potential of Hawkins' invention and vision, she also had to allow herself to accept an unconventional relationship and leadership role in order to see this potential to its fruition. Identifying these kinds of challenges (such as the need to stretch beyond one's current comfort zone and embrace strategies and roles that are very different from what has brought career success in the past) is an enormous responsibility for a leadership team within an organization. In order to realize the mission and vision of the organization in practice, it was critical for each member to discern potential impediments for the team, including their own preconceptions and implicit theories of leadership.

Rather than holding on to the concept of "A leader leads in all circumstances," Colligan, Dubinsky, and Hawkins permitted themselves to rely on the influence of the most effective person of their team for a given challenging situation (which varied across the three members in different circumstances). That is, the leadership team allowed the member whose experience and expertise best fit the current challenge to step up to the plate and lead, thereby maximizing its likelihood of success.

Dubinsky states, "I never thought about any of this as relinquishing control. I suppose I could have tried to be an autocratic CEO who made every decision by myself, but that just seems stupid. It wasn't like I felt as if I was giving up anything to seek the counsel of Ed or Jeff. It was the opposite. I felt thrilled to have two great resources to work through issues with. To me [the shared leadership team] was all a plus. The tradeoff perhaps was that decisions would take longer, but there was such better quality that, to me, that wasn't really a tradeoff at all and, in fact, we moved very quickly even when we needed to discuss things among us."

Hawkins explains, "We had complimentary skills and we didn't feel competitive. Both those ingredients were important. Each of us had unique strengths, but we also knew enough that we could assist the other partners with difficult decisions. I can't ever recall a time managing our businesses where I found myself asking 'what is best for me' versus 'what is best for us'."

Dubinsky continues, "To me, the key thing here is 'know thyself.' You have to know what you are good at and what you are not good at. I found working with Jeff attractive because I knew that I was not particularly good at the product side or at a market vision. I felt like I needed to team up with someone who was excellent at figuring out the right products. [The idea of unconventional leadership structure] makes it sound as if I was giving something up. I don't think I was."

Finally, Colligan adds, "I never really had a concern (about the shared leadership structure) because [Donna and Jeff] were both great people with the greater good of the company at the forefront of their minds. We all clearly had roles to play and strengths and weaknesses that we all recognized and I think we played together extremely well."

The key was that the leadership team committed to sharing responsibilities with those who were best able to get the job done. Each member of the leadership team was challenged to subjugate his or her ego in the interest of moving the organization forward. Individually, the leadership team members reassessed their strengths and weaknesses, recognized which situations best utilized those assets, and allowed themselves to stop being the boss when another team member's strengths were most called for.

Consider a particularly notable example. At one of the more trying times for Handspring, Donna Dubinsky came to the conclusion that the lease on the company's property was going to lead it into financial distress. She concluded that the strain that this contract was putting on the company would ultimately shut down operations. They were in over their heads. While the team held numerous meetings and discussions about the course of action to be taken, ultimately dissenting members of the executive team overcame personal objections and allowed Dubinsky to make the painful decision to buy out the lease agreement. While this decision cost the company millions of dollars, the members on this team of leaders are now in agreement that the decision also saved the company from bankruptcy.

Successful ego management is an important aspect of the shared leadership approach. Yet, it is important to keep in mind that shared leadership is no panacea and carries many challenges of its own. Dubinsky, Hawkins, and Colligan were aware of their relative strengths and weaknesses and distributed responsibilities accordingly. They liked and trusted one another and communicated effectively in decision-making. This enabled the member on their team whose background best matched current situational requirements to have primary influence. The result was two highly successful and lucrative startup ventures.

THE DELEGATION CONUNDRUM

The act of delegation or letting go is a huge challenge for entrepreneurs. While managing egos is one aspect of shared leadership, relinquishing control is another. It is not an easy task. Willingness to take risks is one characteristic of the entrepreneur. Self-awareness and self-confidence are two others that can make the risk taking of decision-making a bit less risky. But these traits can also make the idea of sharing responsibility less palatable. Members of the Palm and Handspring leadership teams were able to overcome these feelings by communicating openly with each other. Ultimately, by truly sharing the leadership of the organization with each other, each leader was able to balance self and team for the betterment of the company.

"While we had pretty conventionally defined roles, I think the magic in the relationship was rooted in the fact that we talked through every major decision with all three of us. We didn't do this in order to adhere to some organizational structure. We did this because we wanted the best possible thinking on every big decision, and there were no better people to give feedback than each other," explains Dubinsky.

As with any organization, the entity evolves over time. The needs and demands of a startup differ significantly from those of the established firm. While the vision and goals of the organization may have remained relatively unchanged, experience and maturation on the part of Dubinsky, Hawkins, and Colligan had an impact on the capabilities of the group as a whole.

In the technology field, the person with the idea or concept that is the seed for a product may not possess the skills to bring that idea to market. Yet, the intimate knowledge and understanding of the technology is critical for prolonged success of the venture. Thus, a partnership must be established between the technology experts and the more traditional leadership/management experts. The often-complementary aspects of their skill sets allow the team to move forward in a positive direction. This is the essence of the relationship between Jeff Hawkins and Donna Dubinsky. Each recognized how they complemented each other and was able to establish an understanding of how they could best support each other as they fulfilled their mission.

The resulting culture and climate had as large an impact on the success of the organization as the product being produced. For Palm, as the company grew quickly, many novel issues arose and the need for clearly defined roles came to the forefront. In fact Ed Colligan's emergence as leadership equal on the team was the result of the obvious need for marketing acumen at the top. Hawkins and Dubinsky recognized the hole in their skill set and found the complementary person (Colligan) they required to address that need. Dubinsky captures the essence of Colligan's contribution to the team, "As the company grew, (Ed) became more and more critical, partly because of his skill set, but also partly because of his strong, natural leadership skills. When we started Handspring, we offered Ed the opportunity to join us. He probably could have gone somewhere else and been the CEO, but he was interested in working together with us again, which we were thrilled about. Ed is a very bright and talented guy. He adds enormous value with his intellectual depth, his understanding of the category, and his amazing energy."

The distribution of responsibilities was a challenge for the shared leadership team because all three were high achievers. The three were full of ideas and capacities, but the leadership structure was designed to allow the person who was most able to lead the organization at that given moment to lead. Eventually, the team developed an understanding of how these tasks could best be divvied up, but initially the process was marked with a fair amount of trial and error. Dubinsky explains, "We each had areas of focus, but we worked highly effectively as a team, consulting with each other constantly."

For more insight on how shared leadership actually worked in practice see Box 3.1.

BOX 3.1—DONNA DUBINSKY ON SHARED LEADERSHIP IN ACTION

Donna Dubinsky was very generous with her time and history in the development of this chapter. When asked for a specific example of shared leadership in action, Donna felt that the team's approach to distributing the Visor, Handspring's first product, captured the essence of the team's dynamic. In her own words . . .

When we were trying to figure out how to distribute the Visor, the web revolution had just started. One of our directors, along with Jeff, lobbied for a web-only distribution model. In essence, they wanted to have us be the 'Dell of Handhelds.' They felt that going into the physical retail stores (Best Buy, etc.) consumed too much resource. The retailers took dollars away with their gross margin, and we had to have inventory there that risked obsolescence and required demand management.

These were all good reasons not to want to be in the retail channel; however, Ed and I felt differently. We thought that the web consumer still would be a minority, and that we simply would have much smaller volume being web-only. We also believed that in the handheld space, customers wanted to see and touch the product before buying. They wanted to see if they could read the screen, to see how heavy it was, to see if they could enter text with Graffiti, etc. We two felt strongly that we had to go into retail, in spite of the costs.

This became a really big discussion, with Jeff on one side, and me and Ed on the other. We discussed, and debated for quite some time. Finally, we arrived at a compromise. We agreed to be web only for a launch period. This made sense to me and Ed because we would have limited supply anyway. Further, we would be clear when we went to retailers that we intended to sell on the web as well (this was still controversial). I can't remember how long it was—maybe three months. But then we rolled out into retail. It was clear very quickly that moving into retail gave us significantly higher volume. But I'm glad we started on the web since it gave us experience there that we needed, and set a tone with the retailers.

INEVITABLE CONFLICT WITHIN THE
SHARED LEADERSHIP MODEL

Each member on the leadership team at Palm brought very distinct experiences, aspirations and personalities to the table. Favoring the creative side, Hawkins did not share as great an interest in the management aspects of the company. In fact Dubinsky joked that on the company's organizational chart, Hawkins was all alone on a separate piece of paper. "Jeff didn't like management (i.e., having people report to him). While he was interested in the business aspects of the company, he was listed separately on the organizational chart because he didn't really answer to anybody and nobody reported to him."

Similarly, Dubinsky and Colligan did not possess the same level of technical savvy that Hawkins possessed (Although Dubinsky happily acknowledges that Colligan did possess more savvy than she!). The complexity of the hi-tech field requires more than the typical personalities and skills of the employee base. The frequent absence of the distinct skill sets that are required to be successful as a technologist and successful as an entrepreneur creates a real problem for companies in this line of work. It is clear that technology prowess is extremely important; however, the urgency of leadership skills and business savvy is equally critical. It is the rare individual who possesses all of the requisite leadership and technological acumen; however, when multiple people are brought together in an effort to provide a complete leadership package, conflicts will arise.

Dubinsky felt this was particularly important. She explained, "It is hard to have all the skills, so teams are essential. In the technology field this is particularly true, as there is a very technical aspect to the work. For example, in figuring what type of smartphone to build, you had to understand various radio technologies, microprocessor technologies, display technologies, battery technologies, and state-of-the-art software. You had to know what tradeoffs had to be made among these technologies." However, the business implications had to be factored in as well. She continues, "If you make the display bigger, you need a bigger battery and a bigger case. How will that impact cost?" It is critical that both sides of the process be represented in leadership decisions.

Balancing these two distinct perspectives was difficult for the leadership team. In order to instill diplomacy in management, all three agreed to discuss major decisions together and would often come to a conclusion by virtue of heated debate. When two individuals were at odds, the third would have to pick a side and join in the debate. Dubinsky states, "We just argued until we agreed! If two people felt very strongly about a particular subject, the third would usually concede. The reason I felt the model worked well was because it drove us to be deep in our thinking. If you have to defend your position, or support somebody else's position, you have to think through all of the implications, and articulate your position. Then you have to respond when someone else points out the flaws in your logic. It's the presentation, defense, and requirement to convince someone of your ideas that allows them to be thoroughly vetted." While, generally, the person holding the losing position was not pleased with the result, he or she embraced the system. Dubinsky noted that she did not believe that their model would have been nearly as successful with an even number of members on the leadership team!

SHARED LEADERSHIP, SHARED SUCCESS FOR PALM, INC.

Clearly, the challenges that faced the leadership team as they created the handheld market varied in both severity and complexity. However, the positive outcomes and lessons learned through overcoming these challenges not only demonstrated the effectiveness of the shared leadership model but revealed several key themes about what allowed it to succeed. The following section will highlight a number of the themes that emerged from examining Colligan, Dubinsky, and Hawkins' use of shared leadership.

RETHINKING THE ORGANIZATIONAL LEADERSHIP STRUCTURE

As stated earlier, the team did not set out to utilize a system of shared leadership. Jeff Hawkins was interested in getting his product to market. Donna Dubinsky was interested in becoming a CEO. Colligan wanted to make an impact on a product design or a marketing program that would change the market. The call of a blank slate is appealing to technologists and managers alike. Creating a product is only the beginning. There are many great products and ideas that go unrealized as a result of a lack of entrepreneurial skills. Beyond the vision, one needs a certain amount of courage to take on the challenge of establishing a new business.

Nevertheless, courageous does not equal reckless. There is a need for a plan. The investment of time and talent to get to the startup point is tremendous and leadership has a responsibility to protect that investment with sound strategy. If the creator recognizes the need for partnering with an individual with greater business acumen, the likelihood of a successful venture increases. In the case of Palm, Jeff Hawkins, as the inventor of the Palm Pilot , realized that he did not have the skills necessary to bring his creation to the consumer market. He needed a partnership with others that possessed the business management skills to do all of the necessary work that he could not, nor cared to, do by himself. Once he found that individual in Donna Dubinsky, the foundation for a successful company had been laid.

The marriage of Hawkins' technological acumen and Dubinsky's business savvy brought the Palm Pilot , and Palm, Inc., into existence. This partnership would not have been possible if Dubinsky or Hawkins had rigidly ascribed to a traditional view of leadership. A hierarchical structure would likely have stunted the development of the product, as poor collaboration could have resulted in each of their abilities being less than fully realized. Their on-going success in a variety of business ventures can largely be attributed to the fact that they did not subscribe to a traditional view of leadership.

Adding Ed Colligan to the mix was additional evidence of the team's willingness to shake convention, as they further flattened the hierarchical structure by bringing a third partner to their executive team. Rather than having all divisions answer to the CEO, the team spread out the key decisions by bringing technology and marketing to equal footing thus eliminating a level of middle management in the organizational structure and flattening the system by sharing the leadership responsibilities. The team took on all major decisions for the company, with each individual bringing their own set of skills to the table. Ed Colligan's background in marketing complemented the technical expertise of Jeff Hawkins and the business/management skills of Donna Dubinsky. When asked to characterize the management structure of Palm, Dubinsky explained, "It was a stool with three legs. We had weekly 'JED' meetings (Jeff, Ed, Donna), where we discussed every big issue that we faced. We also had weekly executive staff meetings that included all executives, including the Chief Financial Officer, Vice President of Human Resources, Vice President of Manufacturing, etc."

COVERING ALL THE BASES

Adding Colligan was a clear example of another success theme this leadership team demonstrated. The team was willing to open its membership to assure that all necessary skills and competencies were covered. Again, each team member shared their individual strengths with the group and thereby allowed the one with the most to offer in a given situation to assume leadership. For example, Hawkins and Colligan took the lead in production and design decisions; Dubinsky and Colligan developed the strategy for product distribution; Dubinsky and Hawkins made the legal decisions and assumed primary fiduciary responsibility for the health and well being of the company. Current research supports the idea of the value of a heterogeneous management team in entrepreneurial ventures. Because there were so many demands placed on the leadership team, it was important that each member had the opportunity to share his or her strengths and experiences with the team. The shared leadership model allowed for such opportunities and in effect created an environment where background and expertise could be optimally utilized.

From the standpoint of shared leadership, the team members' complementary skills allowed them to make effective decisions without stretching too far from individual sources of strength. The diverse backgrounds and experiences provided the necessary pool of knowledge for the team to draw from. The resulting combined capacity created a "super team," able to handle most any situation with a high degree of expertise.

EMPHASIS ON SHARED VALUES AND ETHICS

While there were certainly challenges, stressful times and mistakes, the organization benefited from the trust the team felt for each other. The team demonstrated that shared leadership is most successful when values and ethics are held in common. In describing the dynamic among the executive partners that she has worked with over the past 15 years, Donna Dubinsky highlighted the importance of the "feeling out" process that she went through before committing to forming a team with Jeff Hawkins. She and Hawkins investigated each other extensively. In addition to conducting formal interviews with each other, they each spoke with earlier employers, co-workers and subordinates. By delving deeply into each other's background, Dubinsky and Hawkins were able to establish a level of trust based on common values and expectations. As Dubinsky stated succinctly, "integrity is number one," and she wanted to be sure that Hawkins had that integrity.

Integrity was important to Hawkins as well. The integrity Dubinsky found as a trait of Hawkins' character was not merely happenstance. It was deliberate and nurtured. Hawkins stressed, "It was important that I be credible when talking about technology and the future of mobile computing. I wanted people to believe what I said was credible and not marketing spin. Part of Palms' success was convincing developers and suppliers that we would be successful where others had failed and my credibility as a technologist and product designer was important in achieving this."

In developing an effective leadership team, a new organization must be cognizant of selecting team members that will be able to work well with one another. Dubinsky explained, "For this type of partnership to be most effective, the skills of the individuals should be complementary rather than overlapping." Additionally, Dubinsky noted that there was a trust that developed among the team that empowered and inspired them to push forward. This was grounded not only in shared ethics and values, but in a shared vision of the type of culture they wanted to create and shared goals for the company. They also shared an understanding of the importance of loving what they do and enjoying the people they worked with in order to survive the tests that lay before them. Dubinsky stated simply, "We like each other."

The resulting commitment to one another enabled the team members to anticipate each other's moves and opinions. Further, the entire organization benefited from the confidence and consistency that the leadership team demonstrated.

THE POWER OF OPEN COMMUNICATION

The focus on open communication was not limited to the executive team, but was a value that was espoused throughout the whole organization. Dubinsky commented, "I am big on communication. I was intimately involved in management training. I participated in new staff orientation. By meeting and knowing the people I worked with, our message was shared." This allowed for a consistency in decision-making across the organization.

Employees throughout the system could feel comfortable sharing their ideas, knowing that a well-thought out idea would find a champion somewhere within the team.

Dubinsky's involvement in training allowed her to nurture the necessary trust throughout her company. This enabled the staff to feel that their efforts were noticed, appreciated, and meaningful. The relationships that were cultivated complemented the efforts of the leadership team and generated passionate employees who were invested in the mission and the vision of the organization.

Colligan adds, "Communication is always critical (Even more so when times are tough!). If you don't communicate, people will fill the vacuum and usually that air tends to be negative, so you need to be aggressive about communication. In a smaller team environment, where you built the team from scratch, there is a much higher level of trust, sense of community and respect. The communication is easier and you can count on it staying in the company. I would say it is even more important the larger and more decentralized the organization, but it is also much harder."

Open communication, a necessity in the shared leadership approach to management, creates invested employees—employees who are more likely to make critical decisions "in the trenches" that reflect the overall mission of the organization and protect the organization from incidental failures associated with a lack of quality control or employee commitment. The manner in which the leadership team engaged with one another as well as the workforce reinforced the staff's willingness to invest in the system. The flattening of leadership hierarchy can translate into a philosophy of shared responsibility among the frontline workers. As a result, everyone serves a purpose and everyone is valued for their contributions in both thought and deed.

This makes it especially critical that decisions be circulated among the group. While the members of the executive team at Palm each had their areas of expertise, all three had a say in the final decision. Each member was intimately involved in the decision-making process and the different perspectives allowed for novel ideas and approaches. For example, Hawkins and Colligan may have taken the lead in product development, but Dubinsky was able to add to the discussion her opinions as a potential consumer. The significance of the varied points of view was invaluable.

When asked about the success and commitment of the team to each other, Dubinsky returned to shared values and trust. While the leadership team shared a more intimate working relationship, all of the employees were committed to the vision of the organization. In the case of Handspring, there was a transparency to all of the decision-making and functionality of the company. For example, Dubinsky was not the highest paid employee despite the CEO title—she compensated herself at the VP scale. She held a substantial equity position in the company, so her compensation was tied to the overall achievement of the business. Additionally, the entire compensation plan was transparent. Every employee knew where their salary fit into the overall range of the company and they were aware of the range of salaries at the different employee levels. This contributed to a sense of trust and commitment throughout the organization from top to bottom.

CONCLUSIONS AND LESSONS LEARNED

The leadership team of Ed Colligan, Donna Dubinsky, and Jeff Hawkins experienced great success over their history together. Individually, they are each gifted entrepreneurs with innate management ability and extraordinary leadership capacity in their own distinct ways. Together, they changed the world of technology. The impact of Palm and Handspring is clear and well documented. Palm brought the PDA to the forefront of consumer consciousness. Handspring brought the smartphone to market before anyone else. Both of these landmark developments were made possible by shared leadership.

Intuitively, the concepts of leadership and shared responsibility may seem contradictory in nature; however, the efficiency of sharing tasks coupled with the efficacy of deferring to experts in critical situations make shared leadership a desirable leadership model. This is particularly evident in the field of knowledge work. First, leadership is an active process. It is not enough to rely on the status and authority of a designated leader to determine who leads in a given situation. Rather, to be effective, leaders must recognize and actualize the capacities of those members of the team that can most effectively move the team toward the goal at hand at a given point in time. Second, leaders are also, at times, followers. In the technology field, many of the technical experts are not particularly adept at managing people while many of the individuals with the requisite people skills are limited in their understanding of the product that is being created. Out of necessity, the leadership of the organization must be shared or it will have trouble realizing its mission.

With shared leadership, managers play the role of facilitator as much as possible, and employees are empowered to be a part of the decision-making process. Given the significant complexity of knowledge work in particular, the problem at hand will almost always escape the grasp of any single individual. A flat hierarchy with an emphasis on shared leadership involving close relationships with employees can promote greater expediency, accuracy, creativity, and innovation.

In conclusion, the experience of Palm and its leadership team suggests that shared leadership can be an essential part of the success of organizations of knowledge workers, particularly within high technology, entrepreneurial settings. At inception, such organizations need to bring together individuals with complementary abilities, and who possess the capacity to unite around a shared vision. As the organization matures, strategies for cultivating shared leadership can then be instituted. The ultimate result can be a world class operation that just may change the world, as Palm and Handspring have borne out.

CHAPTER TAKEAWAYS

1. Common values and ethics generate trust and strengthen the relationships among the leadership team that created Palm Inc and Handspring.
2. Open communication between team members allows the organization's mission and vision to be actualized not only at the leadership level but also throughout the organization.
3. Leadership teams, like the one that launched Palm and Handspring, should be comprised of individuals with complementary skill sets enabling the team to handle all challenges faced by the organization.
4. While the ego may create the passion and drive behind the individual leader, for shared leadership to be effective, egos and personal agendas must be held in check and handled with self-discipline and wisdom.
5. The flattened hierarchy created by a shared leadership approach works particularly well in the technology world that Palm and Handspring emerged from because of the unique nature of both the work and the knowledge workers who perform it.
6. As demonstrated by the successful start ups of Palm and Handspring, the effective influence of a supportive shared leadership team can foster creativity and engender confidence throughout the organization.

NOTES

1. Freiburghouse, A., & Dillon, P. (2000). Three's company. *Forbes, 166*(14), 210–216.
2. Hawkins, Jeff with Blakeshee, Sandra. *On intelligence.* New York: Times Books, 2004.

APPENDIX: Timeline

1992 Dubinsky and Hawkins create Palm Computing.

1995 US Robotics purchases Palm, Inc.

1996 Palm Pilot introduced to market.

1997 3Com purchases Palm from US Robotics

1998 Dubinsky, Hawkins, and soon thereafter Colligan, leave Palm to start up Handspring.

1999 The Handspring Visor is introduced to market.

2000 3Com spins off Palm, Inc. as its own company.

2003 Palm, Inc. purchases Handspring returning the shared leadership team to its roots.

CHAPTER 4

THE SKY IS THE LIMIT FOR SHARED LEADERSHIP AT SOUTHWEST AIRLINES

Craig L. Pearce

Professionals Need Not Apply

—Colleen Barrett, Former President, Southwest Airlines

FUNDAMENTAL CHAPTER THEME

Selection of employees is the most important thing you can ever do as a manager.

If you invested $10,000 in the fledgling Southwest Airlines in 1972 your retirement would be set. Today, that investment would be worth well over 10 million dollars. Southwest Airlines is the only continuously profitable major U.S. airline over the past four decades. Just look at Table 4.1 to see how profound the profitability gap is between Southwest and the rest of the industry; between 2000 and 2008, Southwest had a net income of 3.7 billion dollars. The only other profitable airline made a mere 143 million dollars. The rest of the industry lost money, ranging from 32 million dollars

TABLE 4.1 Profitability for US Major Airlines (2000–2008)

Net Income and Loss ($ millions)

	2000	2001	2002	2003	2004	2005	2006	2007	2008	Total
Southwest	*626*	*511*	*188*	*372*	*215*	*484*	*499*	*645*	*178*	*3718*
JetBlue	–21	39	55	103	46	–20	–1	18	–76	143
AirTran	47	–3	11	101	10	8	15	53	–274	–32
Frontier	55	17	–23	13	–23	–14	–20	–60	–88	–143
Alaska	–67	–43	–119	14	–15	–6	–53	125	–96	–260
Continental	342	–95	–462	28	–409	–68	343	459	–585	–447
US Airways	–269	–2,177	–1,646	1,461	–611	—	304	427	–2,210	–4,721
American	813	–1,762	–3,511	–1,228	–751	–857	231	504	–2,071	–8,632
Northwest	256	–423	–798	248	–862	–2,533	–2,835	2,093	–6,001	–10,855
United	50	–2,145	–3,212	–2,808	–1,721	–21,176	22,876	403	–5,348	–13,081
Delta	828	–1,216	–1,272	–773	–5,198	–3,818	–6,203	1,612	–8,922	–24,962

for AirTran to nearly 25 billion dollars for Delta, during that same period—clearly, there is something different about Southwest.

What is behind Southwest's impressive financial record? For one thing, Southwest Airlines is one of the most admired companies in the United States, number seven according to the 2013 Fortune magazine rating. Fortune also rated Southwest as one of the top five best companies to work for. This is not a fluke rating. Southwest is consistently in the top ten.

Beyond the Fortune rankings are some very important statistics from the U.S. Federal Aviation Administration (FAA). The FAA tracks three important airline performance statistics: mishandled baggage; on-time performance; and customer complaints (see Table 4.2). Southwest has earned the "triple crown" in these categories an amazing five times in the past ten years. While their baggage handling errors have creeped-up a bit in the last couple years (more on the strategic decision that led to this temporary blip later), they were the 2009 industry leader in on-time performance at 83.5%, which is 2.1% above their closest rival and a full 5.6% above the average in the rest of the industry. Perhaps most importantly, however, they are by far the industry leader in the *lack* of customer complaints. They received a mere 0.17 customer complaints per 100,000 customers, while their next closest rival had nearly four times that amount and the average for the rest of the industry is more than seven times the Southwest rate. Southwest knows how to keep their customers happy. Ironically, however, and contrary to the advice of pop-marketing books, they achieve this by *not* focusing on the customer. Rather, Southwest achieves this by focusing on their employees, or in Southwest parlance, focusing on their co-workers.

TABLE 4.2 Quality Performance for US Major Airlines (2009)

Baggage Handling Errors (per 1,000 customers)		On-Time Performance (percent on-time)		Customer Complaints (per 100,000 customers)	
AirTran	1.67	*Southwest*	*83.5*	*Southwest*	*0.17*
JetBlue	2.47	Northwest	81.4	Alaska	0.60
Northwest	2.53	US Airways	80.1	Frontier	0.83
Frontier	2.69	Alaska	78.8	JetBlue	0.92
Continental	2.78	Frontier	79.7	AirTran	1.08
US Airways	3.21	United	77.6	American	1.09
Southwest	*3.50*	AirTran	77.4	Continental	1.10
Alaska	4.07	Continental	76.8	Northwest	1.17
United	4.19	Delta	76.6	US Airways	1.44
American	4.61	American	76.1	Delta	1.89
Delta	5.21	JetBlue	74.5	United Airlines	2.37

The airline industry is one plagued by boom and bust economics. Just since 9/11, for instance, four major U.S. airlines have filed for bankruptcy. These include Delta, Northwest, United and USAir. USAir, in fact, has filed twice. Two others, Continental and American, teetered on the edge of bankruptcy but were able to restructure outside of bankruptcy protection. Add to this the minor carriers that have filed for bankruptcy and the list is lengthy. In the midst of all of this turmoil is Southwest Airlines. They, unlike their counterparts, both large and small, have never come close to bankruptcy.

What's their secret? According to Jim Parker, former CEO of Southwest, "Many people think that the source of our success is our pay structure—that we pay our people less than our competitors—but that simply isn't true. The real source of our competitive advantage is our culture, which is based firmly on the principles of distributed and shared leadership." Southwest is clearly an organization that both encourages and expects shared leadership. But how do they do that?

Well the answer is seemingly simple, yet a challenge to replicate. First, is their unique perspective on the *nature of relationships*. This entails the management of paradox. For example, they truly desire their employees to form close personal relationships, but they also require people to fit into a "plug-n-play" type of interchangeability with one another. Below, we illuminate how Southwest does this so well. The second key feature of the Southwest culture that facilitates shared leadership is their *systems thinking approach*. This means that they encourage their employees, from top to bottom, to think of boundaries as blurry; not to act "turfy"; and to consider system-wide effects of actions.

The final component of the Southwest culture that creates fertile ground for shared leadership is their encouragement of *improvisation*. Southwest gives employees considerable latitude in how to do their work. Sure, they have components of their work that must be done in a certain way—for example pilots must follow a checklist before taking a plane airborne—but the last point on all job descriptions at Southwest is to do whatever else it takes to make the organization successful. Below, we detail each of these three characteristics of Southwest, using real life examples, showing how they bring shared leadership to the fore.

THE NATURE OF RELATIONSHIPS

Relationships play a critical role in Southwest's performance. One study of Southwest, American, United and Continental Airlines found that relational coordination—high quality communication among front-line employees supported by relationships of shared goals, shared knowledge and mutual respect—was a major driver of Southwest's quality and efficiency advantage.[1] Even skeptics point to the importance of relationships at Southwest. According to Robert Crandell, former CEO of American Airlines:

> Southwest has certainly done a good job . . . Southwest has become something of a mythology—a love-in workplace. We are on the cusp of that coming to an end; its labor costs are now higher than some of the legacies. . . . When the time comes that Southwest has to raise prices and stops growing, the love-in workplace will go away as well.[2]

It is true that Southwest has relatively high labor costs, consistent with its philosophy that the front-line employees "who have created the most productive and profitable airline" should "share the wealth," as CEO Gary Kelly told *The Wall Street Journal*.[3] But Southwest also has the lowest *total* costs in the industry and is the only consistently profitable airline in the industry.

Still, skeptics like Crandall raise a larger question—are the relationships that drive Southwest's success ephemeral—as suggested by "a love-in workplace"—or are they sustainable over the long haul? Southwest culture emphasizes the concept of LUV, the company has advertised itself as the LUV airline with a heart occupying a prominent spot in the company logo, and even its stock ticker is labeled LUV. People at Southwest really do talk about caring for the company and about caring for each other. One employee explained:

> The main thing is that everybody cares. We work in so many different areas but it doesn't matter. It's true from the top to the last one hired. People tell me—now I know why everyone is smiling here.

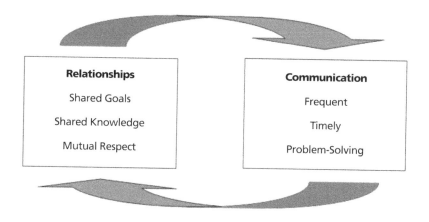

Figure 4.1 Relational coordination.

Personal relationships do emerge among employees in this family friend-ly company, including both friendships and marriages. A flight attendant base manager confessed:

> This may be a cult, but I believe I never had a job where I wanted to go to work. This company is geared for families.... My life has changed 180 degrees from what it was 8 years ago. I have learned to set goals. I met my wife here. I could get real mushy.

But if relationships at Southwest were built only on personal ties, this company's ability to sustain its current success and scale as the largest airline in the domestic U.S. market would be in serious jeopardy. We know from organizational research that personal relationships (bond-based ties) are powerful, but they are not highly sustainable or scaleable over time.[4] Organizations that rely heavily on personal relationships tend to fall apart when they grow beyond a small scale, and they also tend to depend on the retention of a few key people—they are not resilient to the everyday coming and going of employees. But what is remarkable about relationships at Southwest is that they extend far beyond the *personal ties* to encompass *ties between roles*. One pilot explained:

> We're predisposed to liking each other—I like the flight attendants and that guy [an operations agent] over there and I don't even know him. I guess it's mutual respect.

Indeed, a study of American, Continental, Southwest, and United revealed that relationships at Southwest—among pilots, flight attendants, gate agents, ticketing agents, ramp agents, mechanics, operations agents, fuelers and so on—tended to be characterized by high levels of shared goals, shared knowledge, and mutual respect not necessarily between *individuals* but between *roles*. These role-based relationships allow a kind of "plug and play" assignment of employees at Southwest. As the company has grown, employees have been easily transferred to new locations without disrupting the relationships that drive performance. New employees can join the company and become readily acculturated because relationships are not dependent on who likes whom, but rather are woven into the fabric of the company.

Role-based relationships do seem to form a fertile ground for the growth of personal relationships, but it is the role-based relationships rather than the personal relationships that enable Southwest's sustained success over time. The bottom line is that Southwest's "love-in workplace" is far more sustainable and scalable than skeptics would expect.

SYSTEMS THINKING

In a company where tasks are highly interdependent across multiple functions—as in airlines where flight departures are carried out by multiple functional groups under strict time constraints—shared leadership would be total chaos in the absence of relational coordination. For leadership to be shared with front-line employees, those employees need to be on the same page.

Relationships of shared goals, shared knowledge and mutual respect help to connect employees from disparate functions across the organization into a tightly coordinated well-functioning unit, discouraging "turfiness" and giving rise instead to systems thinking. This systems thinking helps front-line workers to work together across functional boundaries to get the planes out on time, safely, with satisfied customers and their baggage onboard. A pilot explained:

> Everyone knows exactly what to do...Each part has a great relationship with the rest... There are no great secrets. Every part is just as important as the rest. The lavs included. Everyone knows what everyone else is doing.

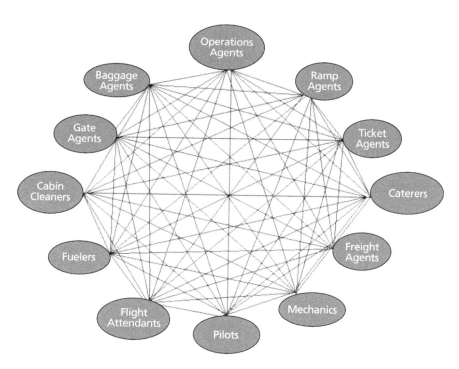

Figure 4.2 Coordinating flight departures through relational coordination.

This systems thinking is not found only among front-line workers at Southwest. Systems thinking is also found among members of the top management team; between managers, workers and their unions; and even between Southwest and its key supply partners—airports, air traffic control, Boeing—perhaps even with Wall Street investors—allowing leadership at Southwest to be shared broadly.

TOP MANAGEMENT TEAM

At Southwest's top management team meetings, managers from different functional areas tend to build upon each other's thoughts and speak knowledgeably about issues far beyond the functional expertise suggested by their titles. Colleen Barrett, former president of Southwest, pointed out at the start of one meeting:

> Titles mean very little here. Most people overlap in functionality. You would not get an accurate impression from interviewing us individually about our areas of functional expertise.

Walking into one of these meetings is like walking into an ongoing, evolving conversation that these managers have been engaged in for many years. This ongoing conversation among members of the top management team appears to be one way in which Southwest achieves shared goals, shared knowledge and mutual respect across functional boundaries.

Scholars have explored the dynamics of top management team decision-making.[5] The value of real-time communication is clear. But it's also clear that meetings are an expenditure of valuable management time. How can Southwest, with its focus on efficiency, justify such an expenditure of time? First, the time invested in developing shared goals, shared knowledge, and mutual respect among top managers may actually save time in the long run by resolving early on the functional disputes that can slow down implementation and blunt the effectiveness of policies even after they are implemented. Secondly, coordination achieved at the top of the company may translate into coordination at the front-line where customer service is delivered. In other words, shared leadership at the top facilitates shared leadership at the front-line, where the payoff in quality and efficiency performance is evident.

LABOR/MANAGEMENT RELATIONS

Systems-thinking is found at Southwest among front-line workers and among members of the top management team. But it's even found to some extent in labor/management relations at Southwest. Southwest is a highly unionized company with 86% of its workers represented by unions, a higher percentage than any other U.S. airline. Despite some fluctuations over time in the unions that represent Southwest employees, its labor management relations have been highly cooperative on the whole with only one strike in its history, in the early 1980s by the mechanics union. According to Southwest's former president Colleen Barrett: "We bring them in here and treat them like family, like we are working on something together, like we do with everybody." This approach has enabled Southwest to extend shared leadership to its unions at the local level as well as at the national level. One station manager explained:

> We have a very positive relationship with the union . . . Union leadership here is good. I like those guys. They support the union perspective, we support the company perspective. Our conversations get heated then we shake hands and move on. If we have a concept we want to kick around, we want to get the unions involved, from a selling standpoint, and also to see if there are flaws.

A contractual dispute between the flight attendants and the company in 2003 nearly led to the second strike in Southwest's history (the first and only strike in Southwest's history was by the machinists in 1983). Discussions at the bargaining table became heated and there was a breakdown of respectful communication. The flight attendants took the dispute public, with picket signs and billboards that asked: "Where is the LUV?" and even made visits to Wall Street to make their case directly to investors. When agreement was finally reached, then-President Colleen Barrett worked immediately to begin healing the relationship between the flight attendants and the rest of Southwest employees. According to Thom McDaniel, leader of the Southwest flight attendants union:

> Southwest has a big party every year in June, employee recognition. It was scheduled for the Saturday after we reached our tentative agreement. People who have been here 10, 20, 30, 35 years and so on get recognized. I had been there 12 years. But Colleen said, 'I would love for you guys [the negotiating team] to come to the awards dinner,' so we all made arrangements to go. At the party, Colleen got up and said that we just reached a tentative agreement with the flight attendants. Some people booed. Colleen said, 'My message to you is that we had a disagreement and we resolved it. We had a conflict but we are a family. Sometimes we fight, but we resolve our differences, move on and love each other.'[6]

In the wake of this labor dispute, Southwest's new CEO Gary Kelly and CFO Laura Wright worked to strengthen relationships with all of Southwest's employee unions. According to McDaniel:

Gary and Laura have tried to create a more constructive dialogue. We have a quarterly labor briefing, when profits are reported. Gary talks, then Laura talks. So many more doors are open. . . . I think the company is back on track. We were asking how to nurture and pass on the culture. . . . We saw more things happening in our management that we would associate with American Airlines. Through that conflict we strengthened the relationship. I feel much better about our relationship than I ever have. We still walk a tightrope between advocacy and cooperation. But I don't think it would have ever happened if 'the girls' hadn't stood up for themselves.[7]

In this case and many others, Southwest appears willing to share leadership with its employees and their representatives on issues that most U.S. companies consider to be strictly "management prerogative." Southwest recently made a bid to acquire Frontier Airlines but made its bid dependent on the ability of the Southwest and Frontier pilot groups to reach an understanding with each other. According to Southwest's press release:

Despite a good faith and diligent effort by all involved, including the top leadership of the Southwest Airlines Pilots Association and the Frontier Airlines Pilots Association, who labored long into the night, the two unions were not able to come to an agreement before the auction deadline. As a result, Southwest's bid was deemed unacceptable.[8]

CEO Gary Kelly explained the company's approach:

We said all along that we would only move forward on this deal if it proved to be the right decision for our Employees and financially prudent for our Company. We have a mission to preserve and protect our Culture and the best interests of our Employees, Customers, and Shareholders. This was a great opportunity that required us to act fast. A lot of people worked very hard with every intention of making this work. We were fortunate to be in a position to examine the acquisition to see if it was the right decision for Southwest Airlines. We chose not to amend our bid to remove the labor requirement, a key reason our bid was not selected. Our congratulations to Republic Airways and Frontier Airlines.[9]

SUPPLY PARTNERS

Southwest is known for reaching out to key suppliers as well, bringing them into a partnership approach that is driven by systems thinking. One of Southwest's key partners is Boeing, the manufacturer from whom Southwest has purchased all of its aircraft to date. According to Barrett:

With Boeing, it's like with everyone else. We try to make them understand that what's good for us is good for them. When you are the launch customer for an aircraft there are lots of advantages. When you're as good a customer as we are, they listen. We don't go along with the crowd. Boeing likes us from our history.

John Denison, executive vice president of corporate services, concurred:

We would probably not change companies unless a partner company ceased to be a good partner. It's relationship-driven. If we think a product is good for us and good for our customers, it is good for Boeing.

The process of product development between Southwest and Boeing was reportedly one of give and take. According to one of Southwest's chief pilots:

It's very unstructured. I don't mean it to sound bad. It's a good thing. There's a lot of free flow of information. The four chief pilots in the four bases are involved. Directors of training and standardization are involved and the vice president of flight operations. There's a group of six or ten to discuss issues, but there's also an open exchange between the executive vice president of operations, the head of maintenance, the head of the aircraft reliability program and the reps from Boeing. There is a synergistic effect of everyone passing information around. Ideas go out; people take positions then try to persuade each other. We are quite direct. People are not afraid to speak. You don't see a lot of territorialism.

The same themes can be found in Southwest's relationships with airports, another critical supply partner for airlines. Instead of territorialism or "turfiness," there tends to be systems thinking and the synergies that come from systems thinking. According to one airport director:

At Southwest, they just don't have any egos. I'll go to make a pitch to them and they'll have everyone there from all the functions. The business guy will say X, the facilities guy will say Y, and the maintenance guy will say Z, and they'll all be on the same page. They jointly come to a decision, usually right there in the meeting. There's no ego.

Systems thinking and promoting shared leadership is also something they discovered to lead increased flight safety in some intriguing experiments conducted at the Swiss Federal Institute of Technology. See Box 4.1 for an in-depth look.

BOX 4.1—SHARED LEADERSHIP IN THE SKY—HOW SHARING THE LEAD CAN LEAD YOU TO SAFETY!

Nadine Bienefeld-Seall and Craig L. Pearce

Imagine yourself sitting on a flight from New York to London. Suddenly, while over the Atlantic, smoke comes out of the ceiling, and slowly fills the cabin. People are coughing, having difficulty in breathing and are calling the cabin crew for help. The members of the cabin crew, who moments ago were serving coffee with charming smiles, walk hastily up and down the aisle wearing fearful expressions. A short announcement comes from the cockpit saying that an emergency descent will be initiated, although the closest airport lies at least 1.5 hours away. After that: eerie silence.

In such life threatening emergency situations where uncertainty, workload and stress are high, leadership is of utmost importance in order to organize, coordinate, and control the actions of the crew and to prevent an outbreak of chaos and panic among passengers. But who would you expect to demonstrate leadership in such a situation? The formal leader—the captain—may have very limited resources available due to the multitude of tasks required to solve the problem. Worse, his or her perception and judgment of the situation might be faulty. Imagine for a moment what might happen if the captain takes unilateral control and even though the copilot or a cabin crew member might harbor doubts about the captain's decisions, fails to speak-up or intervene for fear of undermining the authority of the formal leader.

The sad reality is that many aircraft accidents have tragically illustrated the consequences of extreme hierarchical differences within the cockpit and between cockpit and cabin crews. However, shared leadership can improve the performance of the whole crew such that all available resources can be used without undermining the authority of the formal leader, who still has the last say and holds the final responsibility. A senior captain of a successful European Airline states: "I need to be able to count on each one of my crew members, be it in the cockpit or in the cabin. I may have more experience but I am only human and they are well trained professionals. In the old days captains believed they were the masters of the sky and when I was a young copilot all I could do was pull the gear up and then shut up," he laughs, "nowadays it's all about trust in your crew—you can't do it all by yourself. They need to back you up or take over if needed. That's why empowerment of each crew member is so important for flight safety."

Over the past two decades many airlines have purposefully been focusing on shared leadership for flight safety by empowering their crew members through CRM (Crew Resource Management) training. An ongoing study carried out by the Swiss Federal Institute of Technology in Zurich is putting the concept of shared leadership to the test by observing the behavior of cockpit and cabin crews during a simulation of the above mentioned emergency situation. Early results indicate that the highest performing crews are the ones that share leadership the most fully, while low performing crews tend to either be dominated by hierarchical leadership or simply display a lack of leadership: Shared leadership improves crew performance and increases flight safety. The results are clearly echoed by the results observed when USAirways flight struck a flock of birds and crash landed into the Hudson River in New York City in January of 2009. Captain Sully was very clear that they saved life and limb only through the combined efforts of all of the crew (as well as the efforts of some on the ground and in the river) working seamlessly together to share the lead.

PARTNERING WITH WALL STREET?

One might expect that the most consistently profitable U.S. airline would be well loved by Wall Street. But in fact it has been a challenging relationship. Despite receiving frequent requests to fly to new cities or add new routes, Southwest has attempted a disciplined approach to growth, striving to grow in a sustainable way without taking on more employees or aircraft than they can confidently utilize. Due to this approach, Southwest has been able to avoid the boom and bust cycles that many airlines experience due to the strong link between the business cycle and air travel demand, and remarkably, they have been able to avoid employee layoffs throughout their history. This growth strategy is supported by a financial strategy that is notably conservative relative to the rest of the industry, particularly since the late 1980s when the leveraged buyout movement made high levels of leverage fashionable. In the face of these trends, Southwest has maintained consistently lower debt/equity ratios than the rest of the industry.

But Southwest's conservative approach has met active resistance from the Wall Street investment community. According to one station manager:

> It is nothing new with Southwest. The 'experts' always think we need to expand at a more rapid pace. What these so-called experts express is their desire for Southwest to jump at opportunities at a more rapid clip. Apparently growth excites investors. [But] nobody is pushing us. That could never happen.

Analysts have actually complained that Southwest's balance sheet is "too strong," although in the wake of September 11th and amidst the ensuing crisis in the airline industry, one analyst pointed out that "when times are tough, they have a lot more flexibility." Post-September 11th, Southwest was the only major airline other than Alaska that avoided layoffs altogether, saying that it was more important to protect the jobs of employees, even though financial losses were sustained. As a result of its financial reserves and its ability to therefore avoid layoffs and reductions in its schedule, Southwest experienced the most rapid bounce-back of any carrier in the U.S. industry following September 11.[10]

Still, when the rest of the airline industry began to recover in 2006 Wall Street quickly bid up their stocks relative to Southwest's. According to *The Wall Street Journal*:[11]

> The airline most often viewed as the strongest, healthiest and best-run of the pack may be one of the weaker bets for investors hoping to profit from a budding turnaround in the industry. A strengthening market has sent some beleaguered airline stocks soaring in recent months, but shares in industry stalwart Southwest Airlines have been more sluggish. In the past year, the stock of American Airlines parent AMR Corp. has risen 168% on the New York Stock Exchange. Rival hub-and-spoke carrier Continental Airlines saw its stock price jump 142% on the Big Board during the 12-month period. But the same tide of good news has lifted Southwest's stock just 25% on the NYSE, though that gain still handily outpaced the Dow Jones Industrial Average, which was up 7% over the same period.
>
> The irony is, Southwest's reliable financial strength and reputation for industry leadership have become a drag for its stock. As the industry's Steady Eddie, it just doesn't have the investment sex appeal of other down-on-their-luck airlines that are finally beginning to pull themselves out of the abyss.

In recent years, Southwest appears to be engaged in a more proactive relationship with Wall Street, keeping the investment community well informed of Southwest's plans and intentions. We speculate that Southwest may be striving to extend its systems thinking approach to include the investment community. Rather than doing battle with it, Southwest's leaders are striving instead to persuade this community that what's good for Southwest is also good for Wall Street. With the most consistent profitability of any U.S. airline, this should be an easy case to make, but given Wall Street's ability to profit from volatility, making the case for steady growth and stability is a challenge.

IMPROVISATION

Providing the core knowledge of the business enables what Southwest really wants: Improvisation. Employees are encouraged to do whatever it takes to provide, what they call, "Positively Outrageous Service" (POS). Take for instance, the following excerpts from a couple of their employment advertisements:

- If you want to have fun, this is the place to work! This is a place where you can be yourself, where it's okay to be irreverent...

- We at Southwest Airlines foster and embrace fun, creativity, individuality and empowerment. We love our employees. We trust our employees.

One ad perhaps went the furthest in communicating their desire for people "to color outside the lines," in the words of Colleen Barrett, former President of Southwest. It stated "Professionals need not apply." The message they try to convey in the employment ads is that they are a different place to work, one where initiative and improvisation are valued.

If you've flown on a Southwest flight you know that it is a different place to work. You do not simply receive the industry standard treatment. Flight attendants, for example, often take individualized approaches to their work. It is not at all uncommon to hear a joke or two over the public address system on the plane, as passengers are settling in for a flight. What caught the notice of the Department of Transportation, however, was that some enterprising flight attendants had begun to actually *sing* the safety information during the pre-departure preparation of flights. The DOT thought this to be unprofessional and subsequently called then CEO Herb Kelleher to account for, and stop, this abhorrent behavior. And his response was shocking to the DOT—but not to the employees of Southwest Airlines. He simply stated that he trusted employees to do a good job, that they got to decide how that would be achieved and that he thought it was more likely that passengers would pay attention to such a creative approach to sharing safety information. The DOT backed down. This is but one incident but it categorically demonstrates how far Southwest goes to encourage the improvisation of the workforce. On the other hand, see Box 4.2 on United Airlines, to see the detrimental effect of discouraging any potential for improvisation and shared leadership.

As another example of improvisation, Kelleher recalls, "A guy calls our Dallas reservation center from St. Louis, and he tells the reservation

BOX 4.2—LOST BAG ON UNITED

Christina L. Wassenaar

You never want United Airlines to lose your bag. In order to get it back, you will have to wade through a convoluted maze of 800 numbers, claim forms, and airline schedules all while they survey you to find out how well they are servicing your claim. The main number to the people who are supposed to help you takes you to a call center in India where ostensibly helpful people attempt to locate a bag on the other side of the world. They are extremely concerned with getting you to fill out a survey at the end of the call on how they did and how well they helped you. However, after three days with a missing bag, calls from an airport telling me my bag was in one place when in reality, it had never left the airport where I had asked *for it not to be delivered*, a United employee honestly said: "We get this all the time. A lot of our call centers are in India. They're in a different country; a different world; a world away. People call and are told all the time that their bag is in one place but when I check, I find that they are really in a different place. They don't understand and they don't care." Quote 11:05 pm Friday, Montreal, August 6, 2010.

The reason this is happening is that many companies judge their call center employees solely on how long they spend on their service calls which, in essence turns the concept of service into a disservice. In addition, when they don't understand what you are saying, they just give up, or tell you what they think you want to hear in order to get the call completed. They are obsequious in order to get you to feel as if they have helped yet no actual help or resolution has actually occurred. The actual ability or desire to help and resolve, while on the surface appears to be genuine is, in reality, only a cover in order to increase customer service ratings at the moment of the call, when the customer is hoping that the diffident United call center employee actually did resolve the lost bag. Yet these survey results are what are portrayed to the public as how wonderfully United treats its 'valuable' customers.

agent that TWA has canceled its flight out of DFW to St. Louis on which his 85-year-old mother was supposed to fly, and that he's very concerned about her coming over to Love Field after having to make an intermediate connection in Tulsa. So the reservation agent says: I'm going to be off in five minutes. I'll pick her up at DFW, drive her to Love Field, and fly with her to St. Louis to make sure that she gets there ok.

Let's fast forward and look at how improvisation and shared leadership emerged immediately after the grounding of all flights on 9-11 and the following two days. This situation left crews and passengers stranded for up to three days. Given the Southwest focus on improvisation and shared leadership it is no surprise that the Southwest crews rose to the occasion and demonstrated real leadership. What is surprising however, are the ways some choose to demonstrate leadership. According to James Parker, CEO at the time, some crews took their stranded passengers bowling, while others took their passengers to the movies. Obviously, these folks read the last line of their job descriptions and did whatever else it took to make the organization successful. They assumed leadership roles well beyond anything required, simply because they saw a need. This truly exemplifies the potential transformative force of shared leadership in organizations.

Here is another incident that I just experienced on a Southwest flight. I arrived in Oakland, California and, after collecting my baggage and I was headed out the airport door, I suddenly realized I had left my hat on the plane. So, I went to the Southwest counter to see if it was possible to retrieve my hat. As I described the situation the person behind the counter leaped into action, as opposed to giving me the typical customer service blank stare and "that's not my concern" attitude I seem to receive at so many organizations. Instantly she called for assistance at the gate. But that effort was thwarted as there was no answer. She informed me that the plane was nearly ready to pull away and all of the ramp personnel were likely engaged in that process. At that point, the best I expected was to wait around for 30 minutes for her to make another phone call. Instead, she got out from behind the counter and actually jogged, up the escalators, and off toward the gate. Five minutes later I saw her at the top of the escalator waiving my hat enthusiastically. I was amazed but there it was improvisation at its finest. Southwest hires for attitude and trains for skills. It is not clear to me how an organization could train people to take on the attitude of improvisation.

BRINGING OUR FLIGHT WITH SOUTHWEST TO A CONCLUSION

Obviously, Southwest's focus on systems thinking and the nature of relationships are not the sole aspects of the company that unleash the shard leadership capacity and effectiveness of the organization. They have made sound strategic decisions, consistently, that have ushered their success. Having said that, the process through which that success has been realized is firmly rooted in their desire to create an organization based on a philosophy of shared leadership.

CHAPTER TAKEAWAYS

1. Hire for attitude; train for skills. At Southwest Airlines, bringing people into the organization that have the positive people orientation and interpersonal demeanor is the key, and the necessary job skills can be taught once they are on board.
2. Don't focus on the customer—focus on the employees. If you create a positive work environment for employees they will naturally create a better customer experience.
3. Form relationships based on Roles not just individuals. Many people have similar roles in the organization and trusting that people in particular roles will do what it takes enables plug-n-play relationship building to facilitate smooth interpersonal dynamics.
4. Don't act "turfy"—encourage cross functional, cross boundary debate. At Southwest, the key is to be willing to chip in to help wher-

ever needed . . . "it's not my job" is an unacceptable attitude in the company.

5. Change all of your job descriptions to include the following as the last requirement: And do anything else necessary to make this organization successful . . . that is the Southwest Airlines way!

NOTES

1. Jody Hoffer Gittell. 2003. *The Southwest Airlines way: Using the power of relationships to achieve high performance.* New York: McGraw-Hill.
2. Thomas Kochan. 2007. Interview with Robert Crandall, former CEO of American Airlines, September 4.
3. Susan Warren. 2005. "Keeping Ahead of the Pack: As Low-Fare Imitators Nip at Southwest's Heels, CEO Kelly Plans New Growth." The Wall Street Journal, December 19, p. B1.
4. David Krackhardt and Porter. 1985. "When Friends Leave: A Structural Analysis of the Relationship Between Turnover and Stayer's Attitudes." *Administrative Science Quarterly*, 30: 242–261.
   Karen Jehn and Shaw. 1997. "Interpersonal Relationships and Task Performance: An Examination of the Mediating Processes in Friendship and Acquaintance Groups." *Journal of Personality and Social Psychology*, 72: 775–790.
5. L. J. Bourgeouis and Kathleen Eisenhardt. 1998. "Strategic Decision Processes in High Velocity Environments: Four Cases in the Microcomputer Industry." *Management Science*, 34(7): 816–835.
   Jon Katzenbach. 1998. *Teams at the top: Unleashing the power of both teams and individual leaders.* Boston, MA: Harvard Business School Press.
   Michael Tushman, Donald Hambrick and David Nadler. 1998. *Navigating change: How CEO's, top teams and boards steer transformations.* Boston, MA: Harvard Business School Press.
6. Jody Hoffer Gittell. 2006. Interview with Thom McDaniel, President of TWU Local, December 7.
7. Ibid.
8. Southwest Airlines Press Release. 2009. "Southwest Airlines' Bid to Acquire Frontier Not Selected at Auction: Carrier's Refusal to Remove Labor Requirement Key in Decision," August 13.
9. Ibid.
10. Jody Hoffer Gittell, Kim Cameron, Sandy Lim and Victor Rivas. 2006. "Relationships, Layoffs and Organizational Resilience: Airline Responses to the Crisis of September 11th." *Journal of Applied Behavioral Science*, 42(3): 300–329.
11. Susan Warren. 2006. "Southwest Pays for Its Stability." The Wall Street Journal. March 29.

SECTION III

DISTRIBUTED SHARED LEADERSHIP

In this section we focus on distributed shared leadership—which in many ways is about power and influence sharing across a system. The primary examples are unique. The first examines the rebuilding of the Afghani school system and is truly inspiring. By devolving power and distributing shared leadership over school matters to the local level they have, in some regions, experienced dramatic results. The second addresses a sampling of some of the megachurches that are dotting the landscape of the United States. The case of the megachurches is a bit more murky. These churches have all developed from the initial vision of a single charismatic leader, yet their sustained success requires leadership transition. Some of the megachurches have taken serious note of this and have begun establishing structures for sharing leadership. Will these megachurches outlive their founders? Only time will tell. Our third example could hardly be more different, as it explores global virtual teams that operate outside of the normal hierarchical structure of their firm—Alcoa. Here again, however, the lessons are similar: Those teams that distributed leadership roles more widely were more successful. Thus, we encourage you, the reader, to consider mechanisms for distributing power, influence and leadership to greater effect in your organizations.

CHAPTER 5

CREATING SHARED LEADERSHIP IN AFGHANISTAN WITH SCHOOL MANAGEMENT COMMITTEES (SMCs)

Habibullah Wajdi and Charles C. Manz

SMCs fostered a significant sense of shared leadership and shared purpose
—Shafiq Qarizada, Ministry of Education

FUNDAMENTAL CHAPTER THEME

Especially in pluralistic contexts, encourage and support authentic collaboration that fosters shared values and allows all voices to be heard.

Much of this book focuses on organizations using shared leadership that are primarily located in the west and the United States, specifically. Nevertheless, distributed shared leadership has enabled dramatic leadership change to occur in a variety of places around the globe. Here, we will briefly describe how School Management Committees (SMCs) in Afghanistan have enabled distributed shared leadership to flourish and for a radical shift in the leadership and governance of the country's education system to occur.

Rural communities in Afghanistan are traditional societies which have tended to resist social changes which are contrary to their strong imbedded norms and values. These, unilateral, vertically imposed approaches of the past have resulted in "development in reverse." The failure of decades of relying on an authoritative leadership approach has led to recent interest among development organizations to create change through more participatory approaches in order to bring about long-term social development. In particular, this case reveals that the essence of distributed shared leadership can develop within a pluralistic environment, when shared values are implemented with inclusion of all voices, and a broad collaborative perspective is encouraged.

SMCs ARE THE KEY TO MOVEMENT TOWARD A SHARED LEADERSHIP MODEL

Historically, the educational system in Afghanistan was based on traditional and vertical leadership models, which were rigid and ineffective in dealing with the harsh educational challenges posed by three decades of conflict. The aftermath of this extended conflict (which completely dismantled the entire education system, and left behind a substantial lack of technical, human, and financial resources) demanded "out-of-the-box" thinking and interventions to help reconstruct an effective and efficient education system in Afghanistan. The period of conflict also severely weakened the social fabric of the country.

Notably, Afghanistan's weak institutional capacity, wide scale corruption in civil service, strong vertical bureaucracy, and power abuse had created severe challenges for improvements in its education system. The system was not able to deliver educational services to meet the tremendous needs of about six million school children in post-conflict Afghanistan. To avoid misuse of power, School Management Committees (SMCs), which are formed through a shared decision making process by community members, teachers and school administrators, are being established in all schools of Afghanistan in a distributed model to share power at the local level of the education system. Afghan schools are now experimenting with parents, community members, teachers, and school administrators, providing the foundation for distributed shared leadership in the primary educational setup of Afghanistan.

Since 2004, the Ministry of Education in Afghanistan has adopted a new approach based on "Community Grants for School Development" which aims to shift the management of educational activities to communities at the school level. In this new approach, education funds are transferred to SMCs at the level of the schools rather than to the traditional hierarchical power holders within the Ministry of Education, Provincial Education Departments, and District Education Offices. In the beginning, the leadership at the Ministry of Education didn't buy into the concept of establishing School Management Committees run on a distributed shared leadership model. However, the existence of the traditional "Jirgas" (which are active decision making forums consisting of a gathering of people at the community, district, provincial, or national level, found in most communities in Afghanistan, to jointly discuss important issues and make important decisions in a shared leadership process) convinced the Ministry to give it a try. Indeed, in recent years national Jirgas have been convened which have helped in the creation of a new constitution for Afghanistan, electing an interim president for the country before elections took place, and discussing peace deals with Pakistan. To test the effectiveness of SMCs, a group of experts began to introduce them on a small scale. The idea was first piloted in five of Afghanistan's 34 provinces. Ultimately, the SMC concept became a successful national strategy that is now being implemented in all schools throughout all the provinces of Afghanistan.

With SMCs, communities are encouraged to share, participate and empower themselves to manage their own schools in order to improve the quality of education of their children. These efforts demand that SMCs work in a participatory, shared environment where all members strive to achieve a common goal of sustainable quality education within their school. If created well, SMC's are proving to unleash tremendous potential for positive change in Afghanistan's educational system. As just one example, according to Shafiq Qarizada, EQUIP Coordinator of the Ministry of Education, "SMCs fostered a significant sense of shared leadership and shared purpose. Consequently, the small grants from Education Quality Improvement Program (EQUIP) generated interest among the community members to contribute at a much higher level (in cash and in kind) for improvement of education than the grants received from the government."

THE CREATION AND IMPACT OF SMCs

SMCs are established by the Ministry of Education (through its provincial and district education offices) through a series of comprehensive social mobilization activities which encourage and guide communities in the participatory processes of managing a school. SMCs normally consist of 7–8 members from diverse interest groups; a school administrator or principal, parents, teachers, and community elders. Since every community member cannot participate in the SMC, the community selects members of the committee through a shared decision making process.

After the SMC members are selected, they must prepare a school improvement plan which is then submitted to the Ministry of Education. Once the proposal has been approved, the Ministry of Education transfers funds to the SMC to carry out the proposal. The finances are utilized and managed through a distributed shared leadership process by the SMC members, who equally represent the wishes of their fellow community members. This model of shared leadership, joint teamwork, broad participation, and shared accountability has resulted in a unique sense of ownership and empowerment of communities. SMCs have not only attracted extra community contributions (about 25–40 %, in cash or equivalent), but are also further strengthening the core democratic values in traditional communities of Afghanistan. The impact of the SMCs is very powerful in bringing about community development as nearly every member of the community is involved in participative and collaborative ways to understand the change process, and empower themselves to bring about social change or reform.

During my (the first author's) visits to various schools where SMCs were established, I noticed that some were much more effective than others at effecting change in their communities. SMCs that developed an environment of authentic collaboration where members were willing to challenge one another in a sincere effort to make the best decisions were the ones who had accomplished the most. In these committees, every member had the chance to argue his point and to offer his/her best ideas for the development of the school improvement plan (SIP). These SMCs followed a strong shared leadership model where all actors had the opportunity to advocate for their points of view and leadership was passed from one person to the next depending on the topic.

In the past, schools were all managed by the principal who was himself managed directly by the provincial education offices, and Ministry of Education officials. Farmers, who make up the majority of parents in rural schools, were never involved in school management decisions before the establishment of SMCs. Under the old system, there was not much incentive for a farmer to visit a school and ask about the education of his children. His illiteracy along with his low-status farming occupation was enough to keep him away from the school environment. That is why the traditional perception about education—educating our children is only the school's obligation—remained so dominant and resulted in the slow promotion of education, especially for girls.

The SMCs reduce the power distance between the principal, teachers, and parents regardless of their education level or social status, and create a participative and collaborative environment which encourages ownership in the education process. In this collaborative environment, the opinions of each member are valued, respected and questioned until common consensus is achieved. The shared responsibility of managing school activities has resulted in motivation to engage for both parents and students.

In effective SMCs, parents are encouraged to visit schools, and based on their knowledge suggest ideas for better learning of children. A farmer-Parent X is now allowed and encouraged to talk and explain to students how fields are prepared, different crops are planted and harvested, how different diseases are treated, etc. Farmer-parent Y who is famous for his knowledge about forecasting the weather (e.g., looking at the clouds and predicating the possibility and nature of rainfall) is encouraged to talk about his experiential learning about weather forecasting to the students in the school. Parents are recognized and valued for their knowledge and students are inspired to acquire knowledge to benefit their agrarian society—a needed match of skills and demand for economic as well as social development.

The second type of SMC I observed was dominated by the personal influence of the powerful or influential members. In these SMCs, that seemed to be significantly less effective, there was less participation, less involvement and little sense of ownership among the SMC members. For example, in these SMCs the traditional dominant role of the principal (as a formal leader and educational expert), and in some other SMCs the presence of former military commanders (for whom the incentive to be in the SMC was keeping their political influence), left little space for the evolution of shared leadership. In these situations, when parents/farmers, or other less powerful members, were asked to participate they spoke very little and would often ask the principals to talk on their behalf or otherwise defer to more dominant and more powerful members such as local commanders.

See Box 5.1 set in the Netherlands for a fascinating example of how sharing leadership enabled a group of fire fighters to out perform a group of bus drivers. As with the more successful SMCs in Afghanistan, effective sharing of influence made the difference.

BOX 5.1—THE SKILLS OF SHARING LEADERSHIP: THE FIREMEN VERSUS THE BUS DRIVERS IN THE NETHERLANDS

Deanne N. Den Hartog

Sharing leadership is not only a matter of having a leadership team in which all members individually have personal leadership skills. Everyone on the team must also be willing and able to share responsibility and to dare to rely upon others' skills and abilities as strongly as they rely on their own. In that sense, sharing leadership makes a team even more interdependent. We saw a nice illustration of this dilemma of individual leadership skills and sharing responsibility for a joint task at a local race between a team of firefighters and a team of bus drivers. Each team was composed of six equal members who knew each other well and all contestants were fit, responsible, and capable. No formal leaders were appointed. The first challenge the teams faced was to build a raft and cross a small lake to deliver a statuette there. The team that got themselves and the statuette to the other side the fastest without getting the object wet would win the challenge.

The fire fighters were used to sharing responsibility and working together to solve the problems they face at work. They efficiently discussed and divided the task, picked their materials and were quickly and effectively able to get to work. They shared the leadership process, two men together taking the lead on the building part of the task; another two then taking over to physically get the team across the lake. The bus drivers, on the other hand, were all used to being independent captains on their own ship, personally taking on the responsibility for the safety of their passengers on a daily basis. However, they were clearly not used to sharing responsibility with equal others and dividing leadership roles. The bus drivers had not even started building their raft when the firefighters started their attempt to cross the lake. They all had different opinions about how to do the task and were still arguing about what would be the best way to approach it and even which materials to use to build the raft in the first place when the fire fighters claimed victory. As this race illustrates there is clearly more to sharing leadership than just the pooling of a group of individuals, however capable and responsible they may be!

One of the main challenges which came to the surface during the implementation of the SMCs was how to organize the committee so that the voices of the powerless, less influential and marginalized members were heard in the presence of more powerful or influential community members. The shared leadership model was crucial but it didn't happen overnight and in many places the transition from an authoritative style of leadership to shared leadership is still in the early stages.

EXTERNAL LEADERSHIP SUPPORT FOR THE DISTRIBUTED SHARED LEADERSHIP OF SMCs

Notably, the role of vertical leadership did not disappear during this transition. In fact, in some ways it became even more important, as a new empowering approach was required from the top in order to create the opportunity for distributed shared leadership to emerge. Without the supporting leadership role of the education minister in Afghanistan, the establishment and expansion of School Management Committees would have been an impossible task. The Ministry of Education had to create support mechanisms to foster shared leadership in the SMCs especially in a context where years of conflict had traumatized the education system. They established support offices both at the Ministry as well as in provincial offices, and hired technical consultants to provide social mobilization and to develop the necessary capacity of the SMCs. Although the SMCs function in a collaborative manner, they are supported and maintained through vertical leadership structures provided by the Ministry.

In all 34 provincial education departments, the Ministry of Education has deployed teams of consultants with technical knowledge in education management, social mobilization, finance and procurement to assist and support the SMCs to effectively implement their projects. These technical support teams help to build capacity in provincial and district education offices, and to empower the SMCs to become self-managed committees.

SMCs ARE ALREADY YIELDING CONCRETE RESULTS

Despite some evident challenges, SMCs are becoming important community based educational distributed shared leadership units which have already demonstrated their effectiveness for achieving sustainable quality education outcomes in many rural communities and schools in Afghanistan. The value and respect for various opinions and the sense of argument for common consensus and for common good of the community have made many SMCs vibrant social education institutions. Creativity and innovation is encouraged not blocked in these SMCs. Allowing input from community members for the management of schools has resulted in creative and innovative strategies that are helping to change the traditional and dogmatic learning environment.

Scheduling summer and winter breaks to allow students to help their parents in harvesting seasons, teacher training programs, mobilizing communities to provide enhanced salaries for the motivation of qualified teachers, and more transparency and accountability mechanisms in managing school finances, are just a few of the many creative examples that various SMCs have implemented through their shared leadership efforts so far. And, in the way of a particularly concrete and dramatic accomplishment, Shafiq Qarizada, EQUIP Coordinator of the Ministry of Education, stated that, "School Management Committees have successfully supervised and coordinated construction of thousands of schools at the same time throughout Afghanistan. This is a task that would have been impossible for the Ministry of Education without their help. This accomplishment emphasizes the importance of SMCs for unleashing the power of shared leadership and instilling a sense of community ownership in the education system."

Shared leadership is alive and well in Afghanistan. And the education of millions of students, as well as the cooperative and collaborative capacities of the population in general, is already benefiting significantly as a result. Despite many challenges, SMCs have proven to be the most successful educational intervention in the development of education in post-conflict Afghanistan.

CHAPTER TAKEAWAYS

1. For shared leadership to develop within a pluralistic environment like schools face in Afghanistan, make sure shared values are implemented with inclusion of all voices (such as the various stakeholders connected to Afghan schools including parents, teachers, elders, and administrators) and encourage a broad collaborative perspective.
2. Provide external empowering leadership and support (such as provided by the Afghanistan Ministry of Educations to School Management Committees) that helps launch and sustain the shared leadership process.
3. Encourage authentic collaboration where participants (like the diverse members of SMCs) can challenge one another and advocate a particular point of view in a sincere effort to make the best decisions.

CHAPTER 6

MEGACHURCHES MAY BE RAISED ON CHARISMA BUT THEY ARE SUSTAINED ON SHARED LEADERSHIP

Scott Thumma, Charles C. Manz, and Karen P. Manz

I see that in Pastor Bill, even though he is the lead pastor, He is constantly looking to learn more through other strong leaders around him.
—Church Member

FUNDAMENTAL CHAPTER THEME

Use shared leadership to lessen dependence on any one person and enhance leadership succession.

Many organizational forms clearly lend themselves to the tenets and practices associated with shared leadership. After all, contemporary organizations face unprecedented change and complexity that require more fully tapping into the knowledge, skills and abilities of everyone involved. However, when one thinks of huge, highly successful megachurches it is the image of charismatic religious leaders dominating the spot light and not the idea of distributed shared leadership that comes to mind.

Megachurches and their high-profile singular charismatic leaders seem to go hand in hand. In fact the image is so strong that they are often accused of being "cults of personality," religious enterprises resting on the shoulders of a "great man" theory of spiritual leadership. This isn't too surprising given the national prominence of megachurch pastors such as Rick Warren at Saddleback Church, Lake Forest, CA, Joel Osteen of Lakewood Church, Houston, TX, or Bill Hybels of Willow Creek Community Church, South Barrington IL. Nevertheless, a closer look at the style of leadership practiced in many megachurches that are more successful over the long term reveals a different story. In fact, we find significant staff and congregational empowerment, motivation based on people discovering their special gifts, and a team leadership approach to living out an individual's special capacities and interests within the broad structure of the church's well-defined vision and mission. In this chapter, however, we focus primarily on integrated shared leadership at the upper eschelons of megachurches as the key mechanism for creating sustainable institutions.

WHAT ARE MEGACHURCHES AND WHY ARE THEY IMPORTANT?

The phenomenon, described by the term "megachurch," includes Protestant congregations with 2000 or more weekly attendees in its worship services, massive campuses, countless programs, and large staffs of paid and volunteer workers. A decade ago, renowned management guru Peter Drucker recognized the innovative and distinctive different approach to religious life embodied in the megachurch model. In 1998, he called attention to them, "Consider the pastoral megachurches that have been growing so very fast in the U.S. since 1980 and are surely the most important social phenomenon in American society in the last 30 years."

Indeed, the past few decades have seen a dramatic rise in the number of megachurches from less than 50 in 1970, to 350 by 1990, to over 600 in 2000 and by 2009 more than 1300.

Presently,[1] there are 4 megachurches to every million U.S. residents. These churches can be found in all major cities, 45 of the 50 states and within an hour's driving distance of over 80% of the nation's population. Although megachurches account for less than half a percent of all U.S. religious organizations, they are home to over 5 million or roughly 7% of weekly religious participants. Additionally, these megachurches garner a vast amount of the media's attention while their pastors have become national celebrity figures whose books sell millions of copies. Truly, the phenomenon represents a major transformation in the American religious landscape.

Since the 1970s the rapid proliferation of megachurches indicates a unique contemporary appeal of this massive congregational form. It has been argued that the megachurch is a distinctive response to cultural shifts and changes in societal patterns throughout the industrialized, urban and, especially, suburban areas of the world. The majority of U.S. megachurches are located in the suburbs and exurbs of sprawling metropolitan areas.

While size is the most immediately apparent characteristic of these congregations, megachurches generally share many other traits. Virtually all these churches have a conservative Evangelical theology, even those within mainline denominations. Roughly two-thirds of U.S. megachurches are denominational, but notably most are functionally independent. Megachurches generally have contemporary praise-style worship, including drums, electric guitars and keyboards, huge projection screens, and robust sound systems. These churches host a multitude of social, recreational and aid ministries. Additionally, megachurches employ intentional efforts including home fellowships and small group gatherings to enhance community.

CHARISMATIC LEADERSHIP PRODUCES THEM

Megachurches often grow to their great size under the tenure of a single senior pastor within a very short time period. Nearly all megachurch pastors are male, and are viewed as having considerable personal charisma. The senior minister often exhibits an authoritative style of preaching and is the singular dominant visionary leader of the church. Indeed, given the rapid and often chaotic expansion of the church, strong centralized leadership based on personal trust is critical to the growth and initial success of the megachurch. Indeed, a 2008 survey of 25,000 attendees found that the senior pastor was the top reason given for remaining attracted to the megachurch.[2] At present, 80% of megachurches are still led by the senior pastor who was the central leader during the dramatic growth. Thus, the challenge of succession looms on the horizon for many of these churches.

However, the megachurch quickly turns to a bureaucratic nightmare for a charismatic leader. The senior pastor of an average megachurch must manage 28 full-time equivalent (FTE) paid ministerial staff persons, and 31 FTE paid program staff persons. Few leaders can sustain this complex multi-million dollar organization on the basis of their personality. Thus, the longevity and vitality of the megachurch rests on the senior leader being able to transition to a situation of shared power; at least with his or her senior team—what we term integrated shared leadership.

SHARED STAFF LEADERSHIP SUSTAINS THEM

Megachurches that rely simply on a top-down charismatic approach often end up emphasizing the church as weekend worship performance, with a majority of attendees feeling less committed and only marginally involved. Over time, however, if the senior leadership is intentional about sharing leadership and cultivating teamwork, the church can grow into a functional and productive spiritual organization. Within the past decade a shared leadership approach in some megachurches has emerged where the visionary senior leader, a worship leader, an executive pastor, and several other staff are collectively viewed as the "lead team" guiding the church and its efforts. Many megachurches have adopted this integrated shared leadership approach.

Upper Arlington Lutheran Church, of Columbus Ohio, for example, has created senior ministry teams of staff for each area of the church. It has a preaching team of four pastors who each use common scriptures and themes but preach the sermons in their own unique ways during the multiple services that are offered each weekend. Another megachurch, Community Christian Church in Naperville, IL, on the other hand, has its team of nearly a dozen worship leaders brainstorm a sermon idea and shape the content collectively. Then, one of them delivers it live and by video to the church's 11 campuses. Even Joel Osteen, pastor of the largest U.S. megachurch, Lakewood Church in Houston TX, commented recently "I have a hands-off leadership style because I trust the people God has placed here."[3] However, this shared leadership process among the top staff alone does not produce maximum congregational vitality. Loma Linda University Medical Center—which is the medical arm of a large religious institution—has faced similar issues. See Box 6.1 for how their new CEO has handled the creation of shared leadership practices.

BOX 6.1—SAME ISSUE DIFFERENT CONTEXT-THE CASE OF RUTHITA FIKE AND LOMA LINDA UNIVERSITY MEDICAL CENTER

Christina L. Wassenaar

Shared leadership has a hard time surviving without the leader. At least, that is what the top management team at Loma Linda University Hospital shared with us, when we interviewed them about their new leadership environment.

Several years ago, the Hospital brought in an outside CEO. The finances were in big trouble, and as a result, the hospital was going to have a difficult time meeting its bills, much less its mission. The board felt that a radical change was called for, and her name is Ruthita Fike. She joined the hospital from the outside, with many years of leadership experience, from many organizations.

Over her career, she had concluded that it was best to unfetter people from the typical style of management from the top. Rather, she believed it was best for her top management team members to run their own businesses or divisions, where they regularly reported back to the group their challenges and results, that they know her door was always open if they had a crisis, and that open sharing of information was always expected. Most of the time, she provided guidance but not autocracy and demonstrated her ability to share her leadership role with people both in public and private settings.

As a group, they decided how they were going to re-achieve fiscal health in order to provide a safe, healthy, and growing hospital to the community. As a group, they talked about the challenges that each would face both from internal and external pressures. They learned how better to communicate with one another and with their teams through various assessments and reviews. They began to realize that while each of them were very different, both in backgrounds and skills; on many levels they all had similar struggles. And they all agreed that their mission was, and is, to provide the best healthcare possible to their community.

Several years passed, and the monster deficit began to shrink, until finally, it became a healthy profit, which in turn, enabled the hospital to build and strengthen its presence in Southern California and beyond. These team members know it is due to their own work and the freedom that Ruthita Fike allowed them. Unfortunately, they also believe that Ruthita will not be there forever, that she might be promoted further, and that once this happens, their new leader might not share the lead with them. They believe that it was a happy fluke that Ruthita was hired, that somehow she slipped through the culture 'police' at Loma Linda and that the next hire to that key position will reflect the older, more traditional management values of Loma Linda. So, they trust their leader, but that trust is not extended to their organization or culture.

It's an interesting conundrum, really. The leader does have an immense amount of sway when defining how a group will work. As does the company and its culture. Perhaps one of the key roles for both the leader and their team is not just the activities of their daily jobs, but also the continuous evaluation and creative construction or destruction of boundaries that hamper human progress in achieving organizational goals.

SHARED CONGREGATIONAL LEADERSHIP
MAKES THEM VITAL AND HEALTHY

Staff-based shared leadership is inadequate to support the hundreds of church programs or attend to the pastoral care of thousands of attendees in a megachurch. Megachurches must rely on a sizable percentage of its attendees to not just participate but also to share the leadership and pastoral care of the entire congregation. As one of the lead pastors of Community Christian described it, "We are a congregation that works at involving lay people in ministry." Everyone at Community has an attitude that they need to be training other people to reproduce their ministry efforts, yet these efforts are in their infancy.

Contemporary suburban megachurch attendees on average are highly educated, individualistic, consumer-oriented, middle class professionals, who are also seeking spiritual meaning in their lives.[4] They want to commit to a vision, a purpose, greater than themselves, but they want to do it on their terms, in a way that fits their needs and uses their individual gifts and skills. They don't want to obey, surrender, and conform to the singular spiritual authority's direction. Rather, they want to work with, enhance, and expand a vision they find meaningful.

Very few megachurches wholeheartedly embody a culture of congregationally shared leadership. However, some have made some strides toward embracing this ideal. One congregation is an exemplar. Hosanna Lutheran, in Lakeview MN is impressive in its shared leadership throughout the congregation. Its senior pastor, Bill Bohline, is modest when he talks about the history and growth of Hosanna to over 5000 in 25 years, attributing the growth to a team of gifted pastors—integrated shared leadership at the top. Church members echo this in their assessment of his style, "I see that in Pastor Bill, even though he is our lead pastor, he is constantly looking to learn more through other strong leaders around him." This particular church promotes comprehensive shared leadership through a program that encourages all attendees to take a "spiritual gifts" test, serve in ministries fitting these gifts and work with spiritual mentors to create individualized "flight plans" mapping their personal faith development.

Members and attendees also embody this shared leadership at each level of the church's structure. Teams of volunteers take turns learning and leading worship, ministry, small groups and outreach no matter what their age. So, for example, 5th and 6th grade youth form worship teams to lead "children's church" with adult supervision, while teenagers lead worship for groups of middle schoolers, and college aged adults in turn guide the high schoolers in worship. Every one of their over 100 ministries are guided by teams of staff but implemented by volunteer leadership who are strongly encouraged to develop their own programs and multiply their efforts through leadership training and mentoring. As one member commented, "we've always been encouraged to multiply our groups and raise up new leaders." Another leader described her situation, "There's five of us (in our small group leadership team) and everybody's taking turns and so I gradually started teaching too. I like giving other people opportunities but its all-volunteer led so it's been a new experience for me that got me involved."[5]

In summary, research reveals that a healthy, vital and growing megachurch requires a committed congregation empowered through shared leadership. To accomplish this, a megachurch needs to:

- Educate attendees not just with knowledge and skills but with the clear expectation that their involvement is critical to the functioning of the church.
- Have programs that identify and cultivate the unique gifts and talents of its attendees as a regular part of becoming a member of that congregation.
- Create intentional leadership training and mentoring programs throughout the church's ministries and mission activities.
- Provide plenty of avenues for attendees to volunteer, to mentor others and live out their commitments in the ministry efforts that best fit their talents and interests for service.

If embodied, megachurch leaders are rewarded with an abundance of volunteers and innovative ideas for new ministry ventures tailored to meet the needs of those doing ministry and needing to be ministered to. Congregationally shared leadership creates participants who are spiritually fulfilled, excited about being at the church, and energized to tell their friends about their involvement with the church. Yet, this remains a major challenge for the charismatic leaders who typically are the genesis of such churches.

The creation of this empowered leadership culture first requires shared integrated leadership with top level staff that is subsequently willing to encourage attendees to become involved in the leadership of the congregation and to compassionately guide them to express their gifts in ways that are consistent with the overall vision of the church. However, a critical part of shared leadership in this context is a willingness to recognize that spiritual guidance and teaching need not be restricted to only a small set of top leaders who are seen as being "in charge" or to simply look to the charismatic leader as the one with the special leadership gift. The vision and mission of the congregation needs to reside in the ministry of all the participants for sustainability. If more megachurches embodied this viewpoint the specter of succession would be less worrisome. The more leadership is shared and diffused to the entire congregation, the less critical a single individual—even the megachurch senior pastor—becomes. Ideally, good megachurch pastors can lead themselves out of a job... or at least lead themselves into a new one that is centered on bringing out the leadership of others.

CHAPTER TAKEAWAYS

1. As successful megachurches have demonstrated, encourage everyone to become involved and express their gifts/talents in the life of the organization.
2. Recognize that guidance and teaching need not be restricted to one visible leader (such as a charismatic pastor) or to only a small set of top leaders. Lead yourself out of a traditional boss role (as many of the more successful mega church pastors have done) and into a facilitator of shared leadership to optimize performance and assure effective leadership succession.

NOTES

1. Thumma, Scott, and Dave Travis. 2007. *Beyond megachurch myths: What we can learn from America's largest churches.* San Francisco, CA: Jossey-Bass Leadership Network Series. P. 6–8.
2. Thumma, Scott and Warren Bird. (2009). "Megachurch Attender Report" http://hirr.hartsem.edu/megachurch/megachurch_attender_report.htm, accessed August 20, 2009.
3. Interview with Joel Osteen from Injoy "Stewardship Solutions" newsletter January 2005. www.injoystewardship.com
4. Thumma, Scott and Warren Bird. (2009). "Megachurch Attender Report" http://hirr.hartsem.edu/megachurch/megachurch_attender_report.htm, accessed August 20, 2009.
5. Comments from personal interviews.

CHAPTER 7

THE ALCOA EXPERIENCE OF SHARED VIRTUAL LEADERSHIP THROUGH PARALLEL GLOBAL TEAMS

John Cordery, Christine Soo, Bradley Kirkman, Benson Rosen, John Mathieu, and Henry P. Sims, Jr.

Trust is a Key Element to Success: Trust of the Team Leader in His/Her Employees and Trust of the Employees in Their Team Leader
—Anonymous Team Leader

FUNDAMENTAL CHAPTER THEME

Trust is the basis of leadership.

Alcoa, originally known as Aluminum Company of America which began operations in the late 1800s, is the world's largest producer of aluminum. They have always been known for innovation—both technological and social. Today, they integrate the two through the deployment of parallel global virtual teams (pGVTs), a particularly interesting form of distributed

Share, Don't Take the Lead, pages 87–106
Copyright © 2014 by Information Age Publishing
All rights of reproduction in any form reserved.

shared leadership. More than 80 pGVTs have been launched since 2004, and the best practices that have been subsequently implemented are credited with generating significant increases in production output and saving millions of dollars in operating costs across the globe. Despite the overall success of Alcoa's innovative approach, their early experience involved a steep learning curve as the teams discovered how to develop their shared leadership. We will cover details of the structure and process of these teams. And, we will show that it is the leadership of these pGVTs that is primarily responsible for their success or failure. We identify both the challenges facing pGVT leaders, and the actions those leaders can take to overcome these challenges and ensure their teams' success.

LEADING PARALLEL GLOBAL VIRTUAL TEAMS: LESSONS FROM ALCOA

A good example of the rapid evolution of distributed shared leadership is the rise of the global virtual team (GVT) as a major feature of contemporary organizational life. GVTs now permeate all levels of most large organizations, from the operating core to the strategic apex of the organization, supplanting in many instances the traditional face-to-face interaction. Such teams bring with them a range of well-documented leadership challenges that stem from the need to deal with issues arising from their geographic dispersion, reliance on electronic media for communication, and employee diversity.

Increasingly, however, even the GVT must be treated as an evolving organizational concept, and it is possible to distinguish between different forms of GVTs that are emerging in contemporary organizational life. To date, much of the writing on GVTs has treated them as global, virtual analogues of work—project or management teams. However, there exists an important, newly developing collective structure, one whose closest analogue is the parallel team. Parallel teams are on-going teams which operate outside the formal organizational structure, and which are typically focused on innovation and improvement activities. Once popular and widespread in a variety of forms, for example as quality circles or continuous improvement teams, they have received less attention than other types of organizational forms in the recent years. In a broad sense, parallel teams are a form of distributed shared leadership especially because they operate outside the traditional notion of organizational structure. Members participate in sharing knowledge, expertise, and authority based on a common interest, rather than their position in the formal hierarchy of the organization, and the teams themselves do not form part of the formal structure of the organization.

Parallel teams are starting to attract renewed interest, in part, as a consequence of the growing popularity of "communities of practice." In its purest form, a community of practice (COP) is a group of people who share interests, concerns, or problems in a topic area, and voluntarily choose to interact with each other in order to further their knowledge and expertise. The power of the internet has enabled these collective forms to flourish and to morph into virtual networks whose boundaries transcend national and organizational boundaries. Interestingly, many of the first COPs were composed of scientists, engineers, and academics, situated in a variety of public and private sector organizations and connected by their common interests. Noticing these communities developing, and recognizing their potential as both innovation incubators and as knowledge transfer mechanisms, some organizations have begun to attempt to find a place for them *within* the organization's direct view or 'space'. IBM, Shell, Microsoft, Accenture, and Alcoa are among the many organizations who have sought to capitalize on the benefits of communities of practice via the formation of parallel team structures.

In Alcoa's case, in addition to spanning nine different geographical locations and in both the northern and southern hemispheres, the pGVT membership is especially diverse; a total of 20 different countries are represented. Though some members of a pGVT may work at the same location, the vast majority of their interactions are mediated electronically, by means of videoconferencing, teleconferencing, discussion boards, E-mail, instant messaging, knowledge repositories, and planning and scheduling tools. The virtuality of the pGVT also means that membership, though formally recognized, can be fairly fluid and dynamic. People are able to join a pGVT relevant to their functional expertise at any time and, though the organization tries to ensure the ongoing involvement of a core membership, members may also drop out or change the pattern of their on-going involvement if they wish. The pGVTs also have something in common with communities. Like COPs, their members are drawn in because they share a common job function or a common interest in a particular topic and wish to share and learn more.

What distinguishes pGVTs from COPs and other types of teams, both virtual and face-to-face, is two-fold. First, the goal of the team is to enable Alcoa professionals with similar backgrounds (but globally dispersed locations) to share expertise, solve problems and develop new and improved ways of working. In itself, this team goal is an elemental form of distributed shared leadership, because of the "bottom up" nature of the leadership that is entailed in these teams; Alcoa's pGVTs have as their specific goal the identification, codification, and dissemination of new operational routines. They are the structural manifestation of a "best practice" program, set up so that functional specialists who occupy similar roles in distributed locations are encouraged to share ideas, discuss common operating and maintenance problems, and learn from each others' experience. Ultimately, the expectation is that each pGVT will develop and codify new operational routines, and seek their ratification (sanctioning) and implementation within the company's operational core.

Second, the teams operate in parallel, in the sense that members have other formally assigned operational positions within the organization, and the teams themselves have no formal authority to act or implement their ideas. There are also no formal sanctions for the failure of pGVTs, as there would be for project and work teams, though sanctions can, and are, applied informally. Members must therefore work around their normal day-to-day functional responsibilities in order to complete the work of the pGVT.

How successful are pGVTs? On the plus side, Alcoa reports that some of the pGVTs have been responsible for identifying and implementing a range of new operational routines, in turn leading to substantial reductions in production costs as well as increased production tonnage. On the downside, leading such teams poses some significant challenges and many pGVTs have failed to reach productive maturity, either stalling at the COP stage or failing to sustain themselves as pGVTs and either regressing to the COP stage or folding up completely. Leaders have had to learn quickly how to breathe life into these new forms of collaboration and sustain their vitality over time.

LEADERSHIP CHALLENGES

Overall, the mere existence of a pGVT entails distributed shared organizational leadership. Having said that, the degree to which distributed shared leadership was encouraged within each team related closely to each team's success. To identify the challenges involved in developing this particular form of shared leadership, we conducted extended interviews with 16 pGVT leaders. These interviews illustrate many of the challenges associated with creating and sustaining pGVTs. Leaders must coach members to move beyond their initial COP mindset of occasionally asking for advice or sharing ideas to more of a formal project team mindset, with the mission of developing best practices that will help the company's bottom line. In most cases, pGVT leaders have very limited formal power and must rely on the intrinsic satisfaction their team will derive from seeing their innovative ideas in action. Distributed shared leadership is a key ingredient in drawing out this intrinsic satisfaction. It is also imperative that location supervisors and managers give explicit permission for employees to engage in pGVT activities. In the discussion that follows, we draw on our interviews to trace the evolution of pGVTs and the challenges that leaders face in attempting to ensure their long-term effectiveness.

GETTING STARTED

One of the leaders we interviewed described this evolution of Alcoa's pGVTs this way:

> This community started...when an informal group of people hooked up on telephone for the first time...It operated like an informal group of loose, but enthusiastic, people talking about each other's plant sites. In the second year, the sponsors really motivated this group to hook up as a formal best practice community. Then from an informal group, we gave some structure to the meeting, discussing issues at various sites on a monthly basis. Next, we decided to ratify some practices as 'best practices'. So, in the last year or so, there has been a different pattern of involvement, including monthly teleconferences and follow-ups. [pGVT Leader #5]

Based on several years of experience, Alcoa has identified typical phases in the development of their pGVTs. These are outlined in Figure 7.1, and show the gradual evolution and maturation of the pGVT.

To get the ball rolling on a pGVT Alcoa convenes a COP to lay the groundwork for the transition to parallel pGVT (Stage 1). After this preliminary phase, they identify and appoint a formal leader, create a template for web-based interactions, and develop a business case for presentation to the organization at large with the aid an external sponsor (generally a senior member of the organization). During this stage they begin to develop capacity for distributed shared leadership by ensuring that there is a core representation from all the main loci of expertise around the globe. Then the team begins to meet virtually on a regular basis and to share data and experiences from their various locations (Stage 2).

In some instances, as we will discuss, there are initial face-to-face meetings to 'kick-off' the community or team. After about a year, the pGVTs enter Stage 3. There, they begin to identify specific agendas for action in order to address key gaps in knowledge or common problems and issues that they have identified. The core membership becomes somewhat stable at this stage, though overall membership fluctuates considerably, with new functional experts joining and existing members leaving to take up different leadership responsibilities. As an important side-note, in some functional areas and locations high employee turnover has been a factor impeding on membership stability, a note to which we will return later. At this stage, the pGVT begins to 'produce' ideas for improved operating routines that then have to be sanctioned by the organization before being implemented in its various locations. Critically, the pGVTs must win the support of managers within the operational and technical core of the organization to implement their proposed innovations.

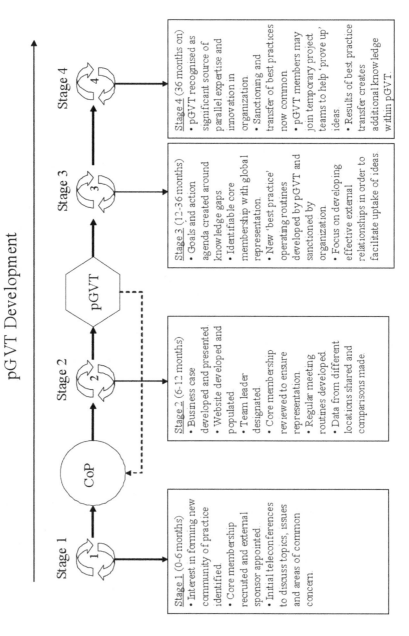

Figure 7.1 Stages in the Development of pGVTs.

Finally, the fully mature pGVT is able to sustain itself as a major conduit of innovation and expertise running in parallel with the main organization (Stage 4). Teams that make it to Stage 4 demonstrate considerable distributed shared leadership and regularly develop and implement innovations across the organization. Team members develop additional knowledge themselves from their experience within the pGVT as innovators, and parts of the team may occasionally join small project teams in order to facilitate innovation or work on a particular technical idea that has emerged from the team's work.

The way that the formal leader approaches early stages of this overall development appears to be crucial. In the first place, the leader needs to take particular care not to destroy the positive and vibrant aspects of community interaction as greater structure and more formal processes are introduced. The tension between the need to find solutions for 'global' (affecting all sites) and 'local' (affecting one location) problems is also a factor here. The leader needs to ensure that both levels of problems are discussed and addressed within the developing pGVT. Another start-up leadership challenge is the development of a compelling initial business case for the formation and resourcing of the pGVT, with some fledgling teams faltering for want of a clearly understood and shared *raison d'être* and key external stakeholder support. Other common causes of failure in early life were attributed to leaders either not developing or following through with regular meetings, so that the team's membership was unable to develop clear meeting routines and a sustainable sense of its own identity and purpose—sufficient to insulate its operations from the pressures facing individual members in their primary role accountabilities.

BUILDING ENGAGEMENT

Perhaps the greatest challenge facing formal pGVT leaders lies in finding ways of motivating members' involvement, in the face of the powerful competing role demands that arise out of their daily operational responsibilities in the various locations. People may recognize that active participation in the life of a pGVT has the potential to deliver significant benefits in terms of delivering operational improvements relevant to their job and location, however, they may perceive that they already have too much on their plate. Leaders were acutely aware of the problem that many members, while attracted to the general idea of involvement in a pGVT, either felt that they were too busy or felt that active participation was not really a core part of their job.

> The first real challenge in this pursuit is that these community activities are an add-on to their normal jobs and in a number of cases the members do

not recognize these activities as one of their objectives. They are there basically because they are interested in what we are doing and to get involved in the broader organization, but this is not the core part of their jobs. [pGVT Leader #1]

This is a problem that is associated with parallel teams generally. However, pGVTs experience it much more acutely because members are dispersed across locations that face different operational priorities and problems, and because leadership and influence must be distributed and exercised remotely via electronic interactions, as opposed to face-to-face.

We identified a number of formal leadership responses to this general problem of engagement. The first involved carefully guiding the team in its selection of focal tasks. Here the goal was to ensure that the team regularly targeted issues and problems that were of sufficient scope that they represented an interesting technical challenge to members, whilst also having broad relevance to each member's operational context. In practice, this often meant the team itself, and not the leader, playing the major role in selecting agenda items. Note that stimulating the team itself to select the agenda (as opposed to top down agenda-setting) is a central and critical element of shared leadership. As one leader commented:

My feeling is that if people participate well then definitely good ideas will emerge. But as you say, you can bring horses to the water but cannot make them drink. However, my feeling is if you make the water sweet and if a few horses drink then others will follow them. This is to say if you make an attractive environment people will participate. To make the environment attractive, I think the leader needs to be persistent. Also he should take caution and should not over manage people. Outcomes fail when people are told what to do. It's a good idea to ask people what we need to do, and get their input at the start. [pGVT Leader #5]

Second, rewards and recognition can also play an important role in sustaining the motivation of the team. In part, rewards for pGVTs come from the more intrinsic sense of achievement that members derive from seeing their initiatives adopted in the operational network and, as discussed later, formal leaders play an important role in facilitating this 'impact'. In Alcoa's case, they also formally recognize the output of the pGVTs, with annual awards being made to the pGVTs who are judged as adding the most value, generating the best ideas, and having the most widespread adoption of their ideas. In essence, formal public recognition can enhance distributed shared leadership in pGVTs.

Other more tangible forms of recognition, such as vouchers and other prizes, might be used by team leaders to sustain member participation:

> Once [a person] gave me a $50 voucher for coming in at night and I really
> appreciated that. I hope I shall be able to provide such recognition to my
> community members. This should greatly help in increasing participation.
> [pGVT Leader #2]

Interestingly, none of the other formal leaders we talked to approved of
the use of extrinsic rewards in relation to participation, feeling that they
were unnecessary if the team task itself was well chosen:

> On the value of reward and recognition in increasing member participation
> and knowledge sharing, I would say that I am a biased respondent on this is-
> sue. I think people should be intrinsically motivated in this work rather than
> lured by something else. I even felt uncomfortable about the [prize] given
> out for [participating in] surveys. [pGVT Leader #7]

Third, encouraging some goal-setting can help to motivate and sustain
effort. Here again, experience suggests that it is important for the team to
self-set a limited number of specific, but achievable, goals as opposed to
these being imposed by the designated leader. Again, bottom-up team goal-
setting is an example of distributed shared leadership.

In a general sense, then, the sense of engagement experienced by pGVT
members is dependent on them perceiving clear organizational and leader
support for what they do. However, engagement also requires energy investment and, as we now discuss, formal leaders can help greatly by ensuring
that the time demands of pGVT involvement are kept at manageable levels.

FINDING TIME

Another major leadership challenge that we identified had to do with being
able to find ways to fit the parallel work in without burning out pGVT members. Since the work of the pGVT is overlaid on an existing full set of functional responsibilities, it naturally tends to extend normal working hours.
Team members report that the majority of pGVT work takes place off the
normal clock, which can be quite inconvenient and has a negative effect on
attendance. Working across time zones due to geographical dispersion, particularly when communications are constrained in certain location, adds to
the complexity. As one leader commented:

> We have all our meetings in the early hours of the day for Atlantic [north-
> ern hemisphere] members and late in the night for people in WA [Western
> Australia]. The reason is that in most of the third world countries, people do
> not have access to international calls at home. This is one reason for non-
> attendance of some members. Other reasons include people are sometimes

overly busy in their plant priorities. In such cases people sometimes do send their proxies but they invariably cannot tell the whole story as well (as compared to the original member). Another issue is that our local WA guys travel a lot and a number of times we have had to postpone the meetings, which is not good either. This sometimes annoys people. In one instance, I could send the e-mail regarding meeting cancellation on the same day. All the WA blokes knew that the meeting was cancelled. In some locations (where it was night time) team members could not learn about the cancellation. One [location] guy was quite furious as he had to come at 6:00 am in the morning... People also get offended when they attend the meeting and there is a poor turnout. [pGVT Leader #6]

Experienced pGVT leaders report several strategies for overcoming coordination problems. First, they attempt to make the virtual meetings efficient by focusing on a limited number of agenda items and asking participants to take responsibility for some pre-meeting work when necessary.

Prior to the meeting I keep on probing people to raise issues/topics of interests to them and on that basis we decide the particulars (who/what) of the presentation in the upcoming meeting. There is lot more activities which go on prior to the meeting in preparation of these presentations. We coalesce and compare data from different sites, and do some research. [pGVT Leader #7]

Second, they inject some basic structure into the life of the team, by virtue of creating manageable meeting routines.

(In) a typical meeting, twenty four hours before the meeting I issue the agenda. I think it should be much earlier but just doesn't happen. It should be at least 48 hours before. I also send a reminder 24 hrs before the meeting. So there are two reminders for the meeting. At the start of the meeting I take attendance and allow the first five minutes for everyone to join in. I start on the agenda after five minutes and then there are others joining in, which is a sort of distraction. Jamaica is always late as always there are some troubles in the phone lines there. Though mostly I run through the agenda, I like somebody else to catch up with the talking. I think a strong agenda is very important for good phone meetings otherwise you are wasting your time. This allows people to prepare well for the meetings and talk. [pGVT Leader #4]

Leaders that we interviewed identified the need to try to ensure, wherever possible, that the work of the pGVTs is woven through the fabric of the normal working day, and also the need to try to spread the burden imposed by time-zones differences on pGVT members. Judicious use of different technologies can help with some of this, while careful and efficient planning of meeting time can reduce the time spent 'meeting' at inhospitable or family unfriendly hours.

GETTING SUPPORTED

Nearly all of the formal leaders we interviewed spoke of how difficult it was to work out how to get resources for the pGVT. Resources might take the form of time release for members to work on a task or project, or even some small financial support to facilitate an occasional face-to-face meeting. Because they exist outside the formal chain of command (and budgeting), pGVTs are not well-placed to capture resources that might be essential for their development and survival.

> One of the growing challenges for the communities is their ability to meet face-to-face. I do not know where the funding is going to come for this to occur. We do not have formal funding for the lead-team. We try and meet when the majority of us are at one place. The rest of us manage to find a few shingles and get there somehow. We do not have a budget for the lead-team to meet twice a year, or the support groups to meet at least once a year. So the lack of resources is a challenge, which again boils down to whether or not there is true recognition for the value of work we are doing. [pGVT Leader #1].

Thus, building (and publicizing) a good business case for the pGVTs appears to be critical to convince top-level and operational management to support the initiative.

ENRICHING COMMUNICATION

The Alcoa pGVTs used a range of communication technologies to support their virtual activities, including teleconferencing, video conferencing, net meeting as well as E-mail. We generally found that the use of richer communication technologies enhanced pGVT performance, especially where those teams are nationally diverse. Yet, our formal pGVT leaders consistently reported flexibility and ease-of-use problems associated with using the richer forms of communication technology available to them, especially in developing nations.

> Teleconferences are the dominant mode of communication. We rarely use net-meetings. We had a couple of video-conferences but they tend to be very awkward and difficult. We used these hook-ups specifically to get the members of the support groups introduced . . . face-to-face. Such hook-ups help in making the teleconferences informal, which is good . . . Otherwise as a regular communication tool, video-conferences are more trouble than they are worth. For a one-hour meeting we have to spend 3 hours in the office. Also a lot of time is absorbed in setting up the systems . . . and then returning back at night time. It is very troublesome . . . not practical. [pGVT Leader #1]

Falling back on simpler voice- or text-based forms of communications such as the tele-conference and E-mails creates its own set of difficulties; however, not least among them are difficulties in sustaining interest and attention and overcoming language barriers. Moreover, when team members trade E-mails and phone calls, others are left out of the loop and frequently miss valuable information. Inevitably, leaders successfully work out a range of coping strategies to make the best and most efficient use of the prevailing communication technologies:

> To make best use of the group-teleconferences we make sure that we have all the information in hand. In the meetings, I may ask a particular site to help another site (which needs help). I generally send an e-mail in this regard and they know they will be asked about this in the meetings. This is to make efficient use of the meeting time. Sometimes, there is spontaneity in the discussions but I try to keep the meetings mostly structured. For a typical meeting, I will send the agenda beforehand. In the meeting I would ask each representative to give a two minute synopsis on how they deal with the work mentioned in the agenda (at their site). Also, I ask them to highlight any issue and try to make sure that I am not emphasizing one refinery over the others. I also ask about matrices and calculations, how each refinery has come to a certain figure. I also make sure that all the spreadsheets and data are in front of me, so that I can correlate what people are talking about. [pGVT Leader #6]

Web-based discussion boards were also widely used as a means of ensuring that valuable information was logged and that exchanges between members remained visible to the group as a whole. Overall, the experience of the pGVTs is a vivid example of how various technologies can be used to enhance distributed shared leadership.

BUILDING AND SUSTAINING RELATIONSHIPS ENHANCES DISTRIBUTED SHARED LEADERSHIP

Another frequently identified leadership challenge relates to building effective and trusting relationships within the pGVTs. This challenge is common to all teams, but it is more of a challenge in virtual teams and even greater challenge in pGVTs. In the case of the fledgling pGVTs, in particular, leaders reported having to overcome the issue of loyalties and allegiances that appeared split between the pGVT and the member's physical collocated. At its extreme, this manifested itself in people being willing to listen to what others are doing in other plants and locations, but not sharing information from their own location:

Team members often have their own agendas and it seems that the lack of initiative taking is due to [the fact that] alignment of management directives are not the same across other sites. Each site has its own priorities. [pGVT Leader #5]

Many of the formal leaders we interviewed spoke of the difficulty in building trust and a willingness to communicate openly in the absence of any opportunity for the team to interact face-to-face—even if this only occurred at the outset. In many cases, the leaders themselves had not physically met all the members of their team and this was also seen as holding things back. In other situations, even though the team members had mostly met each other at some stage in the past, this was not seen as sufficient to kick-start the team:

To date we have not really come to problem solving as a group. People are still kind of window shopping and in the process of finding out what is going where and asking for information from members. I think the absence of face-to-face meetings is creating a delay in conversion of some communities from information exchange places to problem solving teams. Even in [plants located in the same geographic region] people hardly meet. Face-to-face meetings would be very good in terms of a lot of information being shared. [pGVT Leader #2]

Slow development of trust and withholding of information often has serious consequences for a pGVT. Members may be reluctant to ask for leadership from teammates for fear of appearing less competent. Similarly, teammates may be reluctant to offer leadership without some assurance that it will be appreciated. And, members are less likely to appreciate who has special expertise on a topic when communication within the team is inhibited. Low trust and poor internal communications keep the pGVT from performing to its full potential:

Recently I have experienced that people are hoarding information. I needed some information from one of the sites to publish here ... and I could not get information for six months, until after his boss got angry and ask him to do so. [pGVT Leader #4]

Accordingly, a critical role for formal team leaders is to create an internal climate wherein members are confident that their inputs are welcome and appreciated. It has long been recognized that psychological safety, a feeling of comfort and security allied to a belief that you can speak your mind and people will listen, is a key aspect of the interpersonal climate of effective teams. In pGVTs, again because of their globality and virtualness, but also especially because of how they generate their product, a climate of trust and openness leading to a willingness to share ideas and experiences is critical. By their actions and the ways they communicate with team members, leaders are able to play a big role in creating, and sometimes destroying, the positive interpersonal climate that can sustain a pGVT.

Most of the leaders we interviewed were acutely conscious of how the diversity of the pGVT membership posed a particular challenge to trust and relationship building. The following quote highlights the necessity of trust and openness as a critical ingredient of distributed shared leadership:

> On improving of trust and familiarity among members over time and the practices which led to this trust, certainly over time people have started feeling more comfortable. They come to know the rewards of sharing knowledge over time and certainly are much open in discussions. In the early days, I won't say anything went sticky but there was lot of initial reticence. This is because of cross-cultural gaps. This may be one reason for reticence. Also political correctness in some countries like Australia is much more advanced than the other countries like those in Caribbean or say, Brazil. So, I will say that the reticence was because of these cultural sensitivities, and as time went by people are getting along well. [pGVT Leader #5]

As the above quotation also illustrates, cultural differences do not constitute insurmountable barriers. Nonetheless, they are issues which require special attention.

A team member at Bosch put it best when they said: "Trust is a key element to success: Trust of the team leader in his/her employees and trust of the employees in their team leaders". See Box 7.1.

BOX 7.1—BOSCH

Christina L. Wassenaar, Julia Hoch, and Craig L. Pearce

Bosch, a large German conglomerate, has intentionally created virtual project teams that span many borders with the goal of capturing their employees' abilities, motivation and creativity. Over time, they have learned that there are some tasks where it is easy for team members to step up and lead, rather than simply have the team leaders assign each person's work. One team member describes the team dynamics of these groups in the following way:

> In an international distribution team, instead of having team leaders delegating the work to us, we had weekly telephone conferences and biannual meetings for three days, where we discussed and decided the topics together. The task distribution was done by the employees themselves, so I could do it for my task. Of course task distribution was

also influenced by the different sites of the company, which sometimes limited the number of alternatives. In general, we were way more motivated than under the more conservative work forms. However, for this kind work it is necessary to know each other, considering individual strengths and weaknesses. Here, the biannual meetings were very important. Also the new team members could more easily be integrated in the teams in this context.

Obviously, there can be challenges with this type of environment. As one team leader explains:

If I delegate power and decision authority to the team, a power vacuum and disorientation might result. Oftentimes the local team leaders, or line managers, take away the additional "degrees of freedom" and this resource is lost for the virtual team. Therefore when I establish participative and team leadership I have to make sure that the "power" I let go is truly forwarded to the team members and is not taken away by other authorities and by the line managers.

Because of this, trust is a key component of distributed shared leadership in virtual teams. One of the most important things a leader can do is develop trust between themselves and team members, and from team member to team member. In this context, trust can be described as an understanding from one member to another that their task related efforts will be reciprocated and not exploited by other members on the team.

GETTING PEOPLE TO TALK (AND LISTEN)

Formal leaders also report that it is difficult to generate and sustain participation in virtual meetings from pGVT members, particularly where teleconferences are used. Of course, team member participation in the virtual meetings is paramount for distributed shared leadership.

The key challenge is to make people involved. It is easy to sit back quietly in a virtual meeting. However, it is difficult to do so when you all are sitting in one room. Also language background is a big issue. I cannot explain something that well to a Portuguese speaker as I can to an English speaker while talking over the phone. I am not saying they do not contribute. They do when they understand what is being talked about in the meeting. I sometimes wonder about my management style for lack of involvement. I set the agenda, whereas I think it should come from members. However, this seems little bit difficult at the moment... In meetings, I try to get everyone's participation by asking questions. But at times you get nothing.... everyone in the room is silent. [pGVT Leader #4]

The overwhelming temptation in such situations is for the leader to attempt to fill the void created by the silent voices:

> Even after such a long period since establishment, I do not think we are really sharing [leadership] well. It seems myself, and one or two others, are the ones who do most of the talking. I set the agenda and repeat it in the meeting. We have some set points to focus and we try to pursue them. If I know a particular site has done something well, I will ask the member of that site to tell us something about it. Let's put this in the agenda. This is to get people started. We are always hearing from [location A] and seldom do the people from [location B] talk. [pGVT Leader #3]

There is clearly a cross-cultural issue here—one that is particularly important to the success of pGVTs as, more than other forms of teams, their success vitally depends on all members contributing and debating ideas.

> In teleconferences only 2–3 people talk. Others sit back and listen. However, these silent listeners will later on send an e-mail saying we didn't say our submissions in the meeting ... and tend to write in the e-mail what they prepared for the meeting. This is owing to cultural and language background. They also ask in e-mails that we didn't quite understand a specific point can you please elaborate on this. [pGVT Leader #4]

Not being able to fully understand and respond to the subtleties of language being expressed when discussing ideas and their implementation was also identified as a common problem.

> In virtual communities sometimes this becomes a problem when you are not able to observe the body language. Also the language problem adds to this dilemma. You can grasp the engineering stuff but it is difficult to grasp people's emotions and sentiments. In such an environment sometimes it becomes difficult trying to be assertive without being pushy. This becomes even more difficult when English is not their first language. Even if English is somebody's first language the culture is quite different. People from some cultures will say 'yes' even if they have not understood. They do not feel comfortable asking to repeat what they have not understood, being in such a large group. Others will commit to do almost anything (quite willingly) in the meeting but it doesn't get done. [pGVT Leader #6]

The complexity of the challenge facing formal leaders in regulating shared leadership in these teams is clearly revealed in the following quotation:

I would say it's a big role of the leader to ensure that same 2–3 people are not the only ones who do the talking, and to see that everyone participates. It often happens that the more knowledgeable people are doing the talking, but this is not always true as in some meetings some of the experts were sitting silently due to heaps of reasons (culture, language, willingness etc). ... I am the chairman of the meeting and try to see that everybody gets an equal chance to participate. However, this is difficult unless you see what the needs of people at different sites are. It's difficult to have a cue about this need without being face-to-face. [pGVT Leader #5]

Issues of nationality diversity and global dispersion, which create significant challenges when it comes to leading all GVTs, appear magnified in a pGVT setting, where discussion and debate hinges not on declaring technical certainties but on the presentation of subtle nuances of idea and the detailed explanation of members' experiences in their various locations. 'Fault-lines' that form readily around shared time zones and languages to create sub-groups are an anathema to such a team and its success and will compound the difficulties it already faces in surviving outside the main structural architecture of the firm. This makes it even more imperative that leaders plan ahead for how they will deal with these dispersion and diversity issues and acknowledge their consequences for the team's membership directly.

STABILISING THE MEMBERSHIP

One of the key features of the pGVTs operating in this context is that their membership is highly dynamic. Changing membership is a challenge to shared leadership, since the trust that stems from interpersonal experience with each other is a key element of shared leadership. For example, one leader reported that

...almost half of the people leave...every year as they are rotated to other positions. When the turnover happens there is a loss of knowledge and the cycle starts again with new members. This also happens in other communities (precipitation and laboratory) with whom we share knowledge. [pGVT Leader #7]

In one sense, some turnover of team members might be viewed as advantageous, since it continually refreshes the energy and pool of expertise available to the team in its search for innovation:

I do not think turnover has bothered us a lot, as the handing over from one member to another is done quite nicely. It's good to have new members on board, especially when someone brings lot of energy. Guys who can set agenda and push everybody that we need to talk about something specific (initiative taking) are most welcome on board. [pGVT Leader #4]

However, membership instability means that hard-formed relationships are broken as a consequence; turnover is experienced as "a bottleneck in success". In these conditions, pGVT leaders must continually work to integrate new members into the group, both on an interpersonal level and also in terms of becoming aware of their knowledge and expertise.

DEMONSTRATING WORTH

pGVTs operate on the outside of the formal structure, and so it is perhaps not surprising that most leaders also spoke of the huge challenges involved in convincing operational parts of the organization to recognize the value of the pGVTs work so that the ideas and innovations they developed would actually get implemented. A pGVT is not likely to survive long if it doesn't make a practical difference to the organization. The role of formal pGVT leaders in facilitating goal and task accomplishment is one thing, but even more important is the role they play in linking the team and its work through other stakeholders and sponsors to the rest of the organization. pGVT leaders are responsible for maintaining effective alignment between the pGVT and the parts of the organization who are potential customers for their ideas.

In part, this problem is one of getting the rest of the organization to recognize the formal status and value of the pGVTs. As one leader commented:

> Until recently we were a kind of community for sharing ideas....we were always operating at an arms length with the locations, who have the final say in whether something needs to be implemented or not. Until we have local support it is difficult to get the work done. [pGVT Leader #1]

For pGVTs to thrive, they clearly need strong and active external sponsors within the organization at large. Sponsors play a crucial role in mediating the boundary between the parallel world in which the team's discussions, problem solving, and innovation occurs and the operational world where these ideas get implemented. They are also crucial in attracting necessary resources, including negotiating agreement for people to commit time to the team's work and facilitating arrangements for trial and implementation within the organization's operational core. In essence, the virtual team leader plays a vital role in communicating and "selling" ideas from the team to the larger operational community. Of course, this communication between team and context is part and parcel of effective shared leadership.

CONCLUSIONS

Parallel global virtual teams represent a relatively new organizational response to the complexities and challenges of the modern world. They are a form of distributed shared leadership that spans organizational and geographical boundaries and operates outside the formal organizational authority structure. Though they offer considerable potential advantages for organizations seeking to leverage diverse and dispersed expertise, we identified a number of significant challenges they face. Shared leadership is about finding new ways to overcome the limitations of traditional organizational authority structures. Global virtual teams are an unusual and dramatic demonstration of a unique form of shared leadership—one that is distributed. Most of all, the pGVTs developed by Alcoa vividly demonstrate both the challenges and advantages of distributed shared leadership that extend across organizational and geographical boundaries. The Alcoa experience is a vivid example of how non-traditional organizational structures can be utilized to enhance organizational wide shared leadership.

AKNOWLEDGEMENT

This research was partly funded by an Australian Research Council Linkage Project Grant.

This chapter is an adaptation of an article that previously appeared as Cordery, J. L., Soo, C., Kirkman, B. L., Rosen, B. M., & Mathieu, J. E. (2009). Leading parallel global virtual teams: Lessons from Alcoa. *Organizational Dynamics, 38*(3), 204–216.

CHAPTER TAKEAWAYS

1. Shared Leadership is not limited to direct hierarchical relationships; at Alcoa shared leadership spans organizational structures and it extends over hierarchical and geographic boundaries.
2. Alcoa uses various technologies to implement and enhance shared leadership; these include: videoconferencing, teleconferencing, discussion boards, E-mail, instant messaging, and knowledge repositories.
3. Trust and openness among virtual team members is a critical element of shared leadership . . . they are they keys to Alcoa's virtual teams' success.
4. National and cultural boundaries present a special challenge for the implementation of shared leadership. Nevertheless, with appropriate

attention to cultural differences, shared leadership is not only possible, but it thrives.

5. At Alcoa, leaders who were effective at shared leadership were found to be better at (1) interpersonal facilitation, (2) task facilitation, (3) resource acquisition, and (4) external vision and alignment. These reflect key leadership skills most organizations need to instill in their leaders.

SECTION IV

COMPREHENSIVE SHARED LEADERSHIP

Comprehensive shared leadership goes beyond the categories in the other sections by combining all of the types in a highly advanced shared influence process. The three organizations in this section—Herman Miller, Gore, and Panda Restaurant Group—exemplify comprehensive shared leadership. They vary in organizational age from over 100 years to just four decades. What they all have in common, however, is a top-to-bottom belief in human capability—that people truly can share the lead. All are industry leaders, pioneers, if you will. That said, none are extremely large enterprises: All under $3 Billion in revenue. Thus, a natural question might be, "Can this type of shared leadership culture work in truly behemoth enterprises?" The jury is out on that one but we believe the answer is "yes." Nonetheless, no one would consider any of these organizations to be small, and the lessons they inform can surely be applied across industrial, national and other borders.

CHAPTER 8

HERMAN MILLER FURNITURE USES SHARED LEADERSHIP TO BUILD POSITIVE VALUES AND CREATIVITY

Stephen Adams, Frank Shipper, Karen P. Manz, and Charles C. Manz

At Herman Miller we believe we can lead best by enabling and empowering others, . . . to take the lead when circumstances call for it . . . something we call 'Roving Leadership'.
—From Herman Miller Mission Statement

FUNDAMENTAL CHAPTER THEME

Value creativity from whatever the source.

In 2001, Herman Miller, Inc. had ridden a wave of growth for a quarter century. The $81 million company of the mid-1970s had become a $2 billion company. Herman Miller was a leading innovator in the business furniture industry, known for its reshaping of corporate office space (the Action

Share, Don't Take the Lead, pages 109–123
109

Office, with its ubiquitous cubicle) as well as its contribution to ergonomic work (the Aeron chair). Herman Miller had also earned a reputation for having one of the most distinctive corporate cultures in America, which featured comprehensive shared leadership. The company had regularly appeared on lists of "most admired" companies and "best places to work."

In the wake of the dotcom meltdown and the 9/11 attacks, orders for office furniture dried up as thousands of companies closed their doors. With the furniture of bankrupt firms liquidating at cut-rate prices, demand in the office furniture industry fell by about half during the first two years of the millennium. Herman Miller's participatory culture and core values would be tested as the company faced perhaps the industry's biggest crisis since the Great Depression.

BACKGROUND: HISTORICAL HIGHLIGHTS OF THE HERMAN MILLER STORY

Founded in 1905 as the Star Furniture Company, the company was run by the De Pree family for more than six decades. D. J. De Pree joined the firm in 1909, and then became president in 1919. De Pree acquired control in 1923 with the help of a loan from his father-in-law (Herman Miller), and renamed the firm in a gesture of gratitude. Even today, the senior De Pree is such a presence that employees speak about the values he embodied, even though the organization no longer employs anyone who worked for him.

One of the principal findings of management observers, including best-selling authors such as Tom Peters and James Collins, is the relationship between organizational success and a strong, well-developed corporate culture. Such a culture permeates the firm to the extent that it is said that certain types of individuals will thrive in the culture, whereas others may not. The culture of "excellent" or "visionary" companies is based on a well-defined set of values, and those values often flow from an early leader, if not the founder. Such is the case at Herman Miller, which has followed the basic values of D. J. De Pree:

1. The importance to the organization of the contribution of each individual
2. The importance of hierarchical leaders surrendering themselves to the superb idea or expertise, no matter where it comes from
3. The value of perpetual innovation to the organization

Not only did De Pree lead the company from 1923 until 1962, but his sons Hugh and Max, imbued with the same values, reinforced the lessons of their father as subsequent CEO's until 1987. The two sons each penned books on the subject (Max wrote two). Hugh De Pree wrote, "Leaders understand that people need the opportunity to assume responsibility. In particular, the leaders of Herman Miller know that those who believe in the values of the company and understand clearly what has to be done will assume the responsibility for how it is done and will be accountable for results."

In 1988, Richard Ruch was selected by the Board of Directors to be the first CEO from outside the De Pree family. Herman Miller had more than $500 million in sales, and had not only made the list of *The 100 Best Companies to Work for in America* by Robert Levering and Milton Moskowitz, but also the *Fortune* magazine list of most admired companies. In 1985, the company had published a statement of the organization's corporate values. In true Herman Miller style, the statement was developed by a number of teams that included representatives from various functions and levels of the company. The "key value, and the one that is at the heart of Herman Miller values, is participation." This was defined as "the opportunity and the responsibility each employee-owner has to be included in the decision-making process to the level of one's competence and job responsibility." Constructive participation was not to be assumed as an automatic process that emerges on its own, however, "Effective leadership is the catalyst that makes participation work. At Herman Miller we believe we can lead best by enabling and empowering others, and by being dedicated to achieving our vision. For participative owners this means we all have the responsibility to competently carry out decisions as well as to take the lead when circumstances call for it—something we call roving leadership—being willing to take on additional responsibility and work in different capacities in order to serve the needs of the organization." Ruch's three successors (J. Kermit Campbell, Michael Volkema, and Brian Walker) have also adhered to these basic values.

SHARED LEADERSHIP THE HERMAN MILLER WAY

Setting the Stage for Shared Leadership: The Empowered Employee

In 1927, D. J. De Pree received a phone call right after the work day had begun. Herman Rummelt, a Herman Miller millwright, had died. Max De Pree recalled the story in his 1989 book, *Leadership is an Art:*

> [D. J.] went to the [Rummelt] house and was invited to join the family in the living room. There was some awkward conversation—the kind with which many of us are familiar. The widow asked my father if it would be all right if she read aloud some poetry. Naturally, he agreed. She went into another room, came back with a bound book, and for many minutes read selected pieces of beautiful poetry. When she finished, my father commented on how

beautiful the poetry was and asked who wrote it. She replied that her husband, the millwright, was the poet. It is now nearly 60 years since the millwright died, and my father and many of us at Herman Miller continue to wonder: Was he a poet who did millwright's work, or was he a millwright who wrote poetry? (pp. 8–9)

After attending Rummelt's funeral, D. J. experienced a change in his attitude regarding working people. He concluded that in their own way, each was somehow extraordinary. The story of D. J. and the millwright has become one of the cherished nuggets of Herman Miller folklore. One of the reasons for the story's resonance is that the company has embodied the belief in the whole person; that people do better when they feel free to bring all their dimensions to the workplace rather than to compartmentalize their lives. Not all of D. J.'s contemporaries believed this. Many clung to the tenets of scientific management, which involves a division of labor between the role of executives and managers (to plan and set standards), and the role of people in the ranks (to obey orders). Those in the upper ranks of the hierarchy use their minds; those in the lower ranks do not. Indeed, Henry Ford, whose assembly line system symbolized such a division of labor, was quoted as saying, "Why is it every time I ask for a pair of hands, they come with a brain attached?"

A corollary to the concept of the whole person in the workplace is the idea that the employee will also embody the values of the company when away from the job. Gabe Wing, who has worked at Herman Miller for seven years, is a member of the Environment Quality Action Team. Wing sees the team as a continuation of the values of D. J. De Pree, whose concept of "being a good steward of the earth's resources...became part of the culture here...and while we don't always necessarily meet those values or live up to them, we aspire to them." This means at home as well as on the job. Consider the case of guidelines and decisions about using polyvinyl chloride (PVC). During the design of the Mirra chair (in 2001 and 2002), PVC had emerged as a key issue. Although using PVC (rather than steel) in the arms of the Mirra would save the company $2.5 million a year, the Design for Environment (DfE) Steering Committee (of which Wing was a member) nevertheless sought alternatives because PVC violated "cradle-to-cradle" protocol for environmental sustainability.

Wing says that at home, he is "renovating a house that's 35 years old....And we've got the corporate policy of 'avoid P.V.C. wherever possible.' That's something that our group put in place seven years ago. And so I have the opportunity to re-side my house, and so I'm weighing the economics of P.V.C. siding versus wood siding or cement board siding. And my wife and I had a difficult decision this past summer....And we made the decision to go with the fiber cement board and not put P.V.C. on our house....I'm very concerned about the stuff that I'm putting around my family now, where seven years ago, [I] didn't really think about it."

The concept of the whole person is essential to the concept of shared leadership. People are more likely to step forward to fulfill leadership positions if they do not just feel like a pair of disembodied hired hands. Herman Miller has a strong enabling culture that makes it easier for shared leadership to take place. Without such a strong culture, the idea of people taking turns in leadership roles could devolve into anarchy. The core principles of the company are widely held and well understood, making it easier for a particular employee to navigate new territory, such as taking the lead.

The nature of the Herman Miller culture and the sense of individual empowerment it represents at all levels can be apparent very quickly to newcomers. Paul Murray recalls his first day on the job at Herman Miller. He was hired as a manager in manufacturing, and "I took my safety glasses off because I wasn't used to wearing glasses back then. And an employee stepped forward and said, 'Get your safety glasses back on.' At [my previous employer's], there was no way [a subordinate] would have ever talked to a manager like that, much less their supervisor. I mean, this was somebody that was their supervisor's manager. So it's a fun journey when the work force is that empowered."

Roving Leaders: The Key to Shared Leadership at Herman Miller

Sometimes one of the best things an organization can do regarding empowering employees is to get out of the way. That requires a culture whose leaders are "open to the idea—truly open to the idea—of their ultimate vulnerability," notes William Stumpf, designer of the Aeron chair. Regarding Herman Miller, he suggests such openness was "the key issue [that] got them to where they are today." At Herman Miller, instead of having the same individual functioning as the leader all the time, people step forward and lead as needed, based on their interest and experience. Max De Pree called this "roving leadership," and defined it as leadership that "arises and expresses itself at varying times and in varying situations, according to the dictates of those situations. Roving leaders have the special gifts or the special strengths or the special temperament to lead in these special situations." And then they step back and get out of the way when it is time for somebody else to assume the leadership role.

More than simple initiative, De Pree wrote, roving leadership is a key element in the day-to-day expression of a participative process. Participation is the opportunity and responsibility to have a say in your job, to have influence over the management of organizational resources based on your own competence and your willingness to accept problem ownership. No one person is the 'expert' at everything. Yet roving leadership is possible, argued De Pree, only if hierarchical leaders act as enablers, Roving leadership is the expression of the ability of hierarchical leaders to permit others to share ownership of problems—in effect, to take possession of a situation. (De Pree, 1989, pp. 48–49)

Ideas can also come from various levels in the organization. "I don't think we're as hierarchical as most organizations," says company chairman and former CEO Mike Volkema. "I think that comes from a fundamental belief that it's not the power of the position; it's the power of the idea. And you can't sit in a room with somebody who is creative; I don't care what your title is; and not know that person has got something to offer to this equation that I couldn't offer just because I happen to have the title. And if you're not willing to create that type of leadership space, then you probably aren't going to be successful in the company."

At Herman Miller, the willingness of individuals at the top of the hierarchy to bow to the power of constructive ideas has empowered organizational innovation. That has meant a willingness to give a hearing to ideas that might not survive in a traditional bureaucracy—or anywhere else. Designer Bob Propst, the man behind the Action Office, argued that, "the outside world is ruthless about embryonic innovation. It is devastating. In its early stages, innovation is very fragile. It is toddling around. It does not know how to stand up, and it can't say anything very well. People can't understand what you are talking about." Therefore, Probst noted, it was important for the designers to have a great deal of latitude, "We were always in what amounted to a sundown relationship with Herman Miller. . . . We were never employees of Herman Miller. We also cut a deal that we had to have leeway to delve into areas that might seem completely outside their area of interest—agriculture and material handling, waste handling, areas of communication, building structures."

That is true in various facets of the organization. Jay Link, the manager of Corporate Giving at Herman Miller, suggested that when it comes to philanthropy, "we want to facilitate it; we don't want to get in the way. We want to give [the employees] more options, so some of the matching things that we do give them more options."

At Herman Miller leadership is shared not only on an individual basis, but on a functional one as well. Paul Murray was struck by how different this was from other places he had worked, "The first team I was on at Herman Miller was one to introduce a product, and I was in production." At places Murray had worked before, the extent of manufacturing's involvement would be responding to commands such as "You now have to make the paint," or "you now have to build this product." In those places, "they had no idea of the manufacturing capabilities." Instead, what Murray observed at Herman Miller was that the Design Team said, "We're going to bring this product to market. What do we need to do, Operations? What do we need to do, Finance?" That first team experience came the "second or third day I was here," Murray recalls. "So it's indoctrinated very quickly."

CREATING AN ORGANIZATIONAL CONTEXT FOR SHARED LEADERSHIP

Shared leadership cannot occur in a vacuum. There are a variety of factors that provide the support needed for shared leadership at Herman Miller. In particular, we will focus on four key elements of the organization: shared equity, sharing the creative process both within and outside the company, establishment of a new social contract with stakeholders, and an ongoing commitment to the core strength of innovation.

Shared Leadership is Supported by Shared Equity

An article about the Scanlon Plan, which was based on the idea that valuable ideas involving operations efficiency and cost effectiveness could originate at all levels, appeared in the January 1950 issue of *Fortune* magazine and caught the attention of Herman Miller managers. The company was still rather small, with a work force of fewer than 200, and annual sales of fewer than $2 million, yet was experiencing some of the problems of larger firms. Although the designs were excellent, manufactured products were of inadequate quality and were not delivered in a timely manner. It was crucial to better align the interests of the managers and the employees, and to instill a group-based incentive. That's where the Scanlon Plan came in. It had three principal pillars:

1. Productivity "norms," agreed on between management and workers
2. Bonuses, based on savings achieved, involving all employees rather than a few at the top of the hierarchy
3. A system of production councils (at Herman Miller, teams) which involve individuals at all levels in reducing costs

Joe Scanlon, a lecturer in industrial relations at the Massachusetts Institute of Technology, had established the innovative approach in the 1930s, and Carl Frost, a professor at Michigan State University, brought the concept to Herman Miller. The principles behind the plan included identity, equity, competence, and participation. As Hugh De Pree put it, "It was a change from 'piece work' and every man for himself to each person being not only responsible for himself but for every other person in the organization."

For another example of innovative performance that enabled a company to achieve a major turnaround see Box 8.1 about Behlen Manufacturing.

BOX 8.1—CAN US-BASED MANUFACTURING BE SAVED? BEHLEN GROUP'S TONY RAIMONDO SAYS YES!

Craig L. Pearce

What country has the largest manufacturing output in the world? If you answered China, and most people do, you would be wrong. The United States of America is still the world's largest manufacturer; it's just that the type of output has shifted over time. And it will continue to shift as the world's economies converge.

One of the success stories in U.S. manufacturing is Behlen Group, headquartered in Columbus, Nebraska, a small town of a little over 20,000. Behlen Group primarily manufactures products for the agricultural industry—things like feed bins, troughs and gates. When Tony Raimondo and some fellow investors bought the firm back in 1984 it had $32 Million in sales, with an operating loss of $7 Million. From those dire beginnings, the firm has emerged as a powerhouse. Just look at a couple of facts and you'll get the picture. In 1994, Tony Raimondo and Behlen was named turnaround entrepreneur of the year by *Inc.* magazine. Perhaps even more impressive, Behlen Group has a record of exporting manufactured goods to more than 70 countries, *including* China.

To what does Tony Raimondo attribute their success? His answer is succinct. "It's our partners in progress." That is the term they use for employees at Behlen Group, and it is not just another buzz word dreamed up by Dilbert-like executives. They really mean it. The whole firm is organized into multi-team systems, each of which is responsible for a particular product from beginning to end. Raimondo, who has turned over day-to-day operations to his sons, Phil and Tony, Jr., states, "We give our partners in progress the autonomy to get their jobs done, the ability to measure their progress and productivity, and the opportunity to share in the productivity gains." While things are going great for Behlen, they are on the constant search for ways to improve—it is simply part of their culture and shared leadership is the underlying mechanism that makes it all happen.

As in other aspects of shared leadership, shared equity at Herman Miller bolstered confidence in the ranks. John Berry recalled his first Scanlon meeting, during which the CEO, president, and other senior officers made presentations. During the subsequent question-and-answer period, the individual sitting next to Berry stood up and said, "The company stock has gone down two points, and I want to know what you are going to do to fix it." Instead of getting defensive, the president responded, "Great question, let me tell you what we know about that, what we think is the reason, and what we are going to do about it."

The Scanlon Plan was subsequently revised several times to reflect an evolving workforce. For instance, an increasing percentage of employees were performing "indirect" activities, including marketing and sales, finance and accounting, purchasing and data processing. In 1983, the company implemented a more broad based form of employee stock ownership. The new PAYSOP program enabled every full-time employee with at least one year of service to become a shareholder. "Around here," observed Max De Pree, "the employees act as if they own the place."

Sharing the Creative Process
Inside and Outside the Company

Shared leadership can appear in an organization in many forms. At Herman Miller, one of the most important means to that end was individuals who had a contractual relationship with the firm rather than that of traditional employer/employee. It was just this sort of relationship, notes James O'Toole, that allowed "a company based in Zeeland, Michigan, a frosty town with no bars, no pool halls, and no theaters" to unleash some of the furniture industry's most creative ideas. Top designers would come to Zeeland, said Max De Pree, because D.J. De Pree and his successors "had the strength to abandon themselves to the wild ideas of others."

In a design-driven organization, the designer does not come in at the end of the product creation process and then add some semblance of style. Instead, the designer takes the lead in new product development, which means taking the lead in solving a customer problem. By defining itself as a design-driven company, Herman Miller was able to go beyond the idea of shared leadership within the organization, and include outsiders in the leadership process. Therefore, the concept of shared leadership at Herman Miller is inextricably bound up with the integration of business and design.

The Star Furniture Company, and then the Herman Miller Company in its early years, had manufactured reproductions of traditional home furniture. In 1930, D.J. De Pree met furniture designer Gilbert Rohde, who bluntly told De Pree that the company's offerings did not fit the needs of contemporary American life. De Pree was put off at first, but then recognized that with the onset of the Great Depression, its current product line might not sustain the company. Instead, functional, flexible, and spare furniture had more of a future. De Pree agreed to pay Rohde a 3% royalty on any furniture sales.

Since then, one of the distinctive aspects of Herman Miller has been that one of its core competencies is design, and design has come from independent contractors rather than from individuals on staff. Even George Nelson, who held the title of Design Director for several years, operated from New York City and had relationships with other firms as well. Mike Volkema explained, "D. J. never believed that the creative class could be contained within the corporate walls. It's a very unique view of the world, but he had an idea of creativity being networked long before we had the Internet, or people started to talk about network economies, or all that." One thing that keeping such an organizational (and geographic) distance from designers accomplishes is that it diminishes the chance that the organization will stand between the designers and a promising idea. As Don Goeman, Herman Miller Vice President of Design and Development, notes, such a set-up keeps designers "at a healthy distance from the kinds of day-to-day internal processes that might inhibit their thinking and prevent a greater level of creativity from emerging."

The networked aspect of Herman Miller extends beyond design. A glimpse of the manufacturing operation in Zeeland suggests just how much so. One of the first things a visitor may note is how modest the operation seems to be; this is, after all, a $2 billion company. Herman Miller manufactures in the states of Georgia and Washington, as well as in the United Kingdom and in China. Just as in design, manufacturing also features a surrender of control. Much of the important activity in this firm takes place under somebody else's roof. What the visitor sees is assembly; many of the component parts are outsourced. Further, the amounts of finished goods in the manufacturing area are quite small; small inventory levels relative to sales is an integral part of the Herman Miller Production System (HMPS).

A similar set of relationships follows product through Herman Miller's supply chain. Most of Herman Miller's products are bought and then sold to end customers by a network of independently owned and operated contract furniture dealerships.

The company coveys to external stakeholders, including customers, its core values, and does this through the properties of its products. For example, during the 1930s and 1940s, Gilbert Rohde provided the company designs of desks that acted more as functional devices than as status symbols—a reflection of the firm's philosophy of embracing the best idea. More recently, the company's commitment to environmental stewardship was reflected in seeking alternatives to rose wood, a tropical hardwood, in the famous Eames® lounge chair and ottoman, long before green marketing and management were part of the business vocabulary.

Herman Miller was and is selling more than a new set of design; it was selling a new approach to management as well. Central to that management approach has been the belief in the inherent value of each employee and that the next idea or problem solution could come from virtually anywhere in the company as well as from outsiders. The company's approach to management has been to embrace the best idea (and its source—either inside or outside the company). Management perceived its duty to facilitate the communication and implementation of both new product, and organizational ideas. Herman Miller tore down the walls of the modern workspace at the same time that the company's concept of team-based activity and broad-based equity reward was gaining recognition for innovative human relations. The Action Office, which debuted in 1968, represented a physical representation of the collaborative work encouraged at Herman Miller.

Establishing a New Social Contract

One thing that employees, customers, and other stakeholders want to know is the extent to which an organization's values are enduring. Will a company embody its stated values when things are not going well? As Mike Volkema noted, "There's a lot of times where you get tested against the things that you say you believe." Therefore, the best test of a company's values is during an acute crisis, the dark night of an organization's soul. During the Great Depression, when the company's future was hanging in the balance, D.J. recognized the potential of Gilbert Rohde's simple approach to design, a departure from the classical reproductions upon which the company had been built. As Robert McClory put it, "De Pree 'abandoned himself' to Rohde, an independent contractor, and his approach." Such a surrender of control would become a leitmotif in the company, whether in dealing with subsequent outside designers, or in sharing leadership with individuals at various ranks in the company based on their ideas and expertise.

Herman Miller confronted such a test in the wake of the dotcom meltdown, and the economic slowdown following the 9/11 attacks. The company responded in two major ways:

1. Adapting its culture to a new external reality
2. Reinforcing its identity as an innovation-based company

In so doing, the company adhered to its values.

For much of the twentieth century, many companies (including blue chips such as IBM, AT&T, and Hewlett-Packard) made an informal agreement with their workers. If you come in every day and work hard, the company will succeed, and you will have a job for as long as you want. It may not have been lifetime employment, but it was certainly expected to be a long-term relationship. Such a contract existed at Herman Miller. Near the entrance to Herman Miller's Design Yard, which houses the company's design studio and executive offices—is a statue called "Watercarrier," which reflects the Native American belief in the role of each task, no matter how humble, in the survival of the community. Max De Pree, who began the tradition in 1987 (first Watercarrier—D.J. De Pree), believed "Watercarriers transfer the essence of the institution to new people." Herman Miller has more than 1,400 Watercarriers, workers who have been with the firm for more than 20 years. A reflection pool at the Design Yard displays all their names.

Acknowledging the reality of the late twentieth century (that global competition combined with rapid technological change to shape a work environment that could not sustain the old social contract), Herman Miller had begun to re-craft its benefits structure. One of the key changes was to provide more "portable" benefits, such as 401K plans and educational reimbursement. Herman Miller employees would garner financial security, and the ability to improve themselves professionally, but with no promise that they would stay at Herman Miller for their entire careers.

Instead, as Mike Volkema noted, the company acknowledged that, "We are a commercial enterprise, and the customer has to be on center stage, so we have to first figure out whether your gifts and talents have a match with the needs and wants of this commercial enterprise. If they don't, then we want to wish you the best, but we do need to tell you that I don't have a job for you right now."

The philosophy behind the new social contract was consistent with the firm's basis as a design-oriented firm. Indeed, in a 1972 interview, designer Charles Eames was asked whether he had been "forced to accept compromises." He responded, "I don't remember ever being forced to accept compromises, but I have willingly accepted constraints." His list of constraints included price, size, strength, balance, and time. At Herman Miller, acknowledgement that the firm could not guarantee lifetime employment was not a compromise of its principles and values, but rather acceptance of constraints—such as the needs of the customer, and the requirement that the company make a profit. As CPA Frank Seidman, Founder of Seidman & Seidman, once reminded Hugh De Pree, "Any damn fool can give it away."

That philosophy would be important in 2002. Mike Volkema, who was CEO at the time, remembered, "In 1995, when I took over, sales were under $1 billion. By 2000, they were $2.2 billion. By 2003, they were down to $1.3 billion. One night I went to bed a genius and woke up the town idiot. It was not a happy time to be in leadership." This represented two to three times the magnitude of any downturn the firm had faced in the previous three decades. "Ultimately, we had to tell 4,500 of our 12,000 employees that we no longer had work for them." Volkema and Brian Walker, who was president of Herman Miller North America, made a point of delivering the worst news themselves, including the shuttering of a plant in Georgia. After the announcement, workers expressed their concern for the two. "I can't think of anything that would rip your heart out more than for these people, who you had just laid off, to tell you that they hoped you'd be okay," Walker said.

"We really worked hard to live our values in the midst of that trial," recalled Volkema. "And I think we did a really incredible job. I know we spent tens of millions of dollars more than our competitor to help transition people, when we didn't have enough work for everybody, to other opportunities." Each employee who lost his or her job was told the news face to face by somebody they knew. The crisis not only gave Herman Miller an opportunity to test its beliefs, but allowed the company and its employees to draw on years of commitment to one another. One of those who lost her job was a woman who had worked as an assistant to Volkema at Meridian Furniture Company before Herman Miller acquired Meridian in 1990. After losing her job, she wrote that her experience at Herman Miller was "nothing but great, and I didn't have a college education, and I didn't have the MBA I now hold…so I walk away knowing that I've got lots of opportunities in front of me to pursue." Volkema was struck by how "even in the worst of circumstances, when a job gets eliminated, that somebody goes away holding their head high."

Staying Committed to the Core Strength—Innovation

Companies facing major crises often make major cuts to Research and Development, focusing more on existing product lines. New ideas are postponed or abandoned altogether. Such an approach can be a default mode in an established organization, where what already exists has a constituency to defend it, whereas what does not yet exist does not. As Gary Miller, head of Herman Miller Creative Office (HMCO) noted, "It's a product of institutions that are successful to create templates for success that ultimately cast out new ideas.…It's press of business and mature market that constrains you to do what you know, stay close to the knitting."

Instead, the CEO and Board of Directors sustained an initiative begun in 2001, with the establishment of the HMCO. The project, called *Purple*, was designed to lead Herman Miller into utterly new areas of business with new markets and new sets of customers. In true Herman Miller style, the *Purple* initiative involved individuals from both inside and outside the organization. One measure of the initiative's success would be the extent to which the identified opportunities extended the company beyond the traditional confines of the furniture industry, through capabilities in environmental enrichment (such as sound and temperature control), lighting (such as light emitting diodes), technology integration (such as wireless capabilities), redefining space, and design/build process (exploring environmental and security issues).

The Creative Office and *Purple* represented among the most daring aspects of tens of millions of dollars Herman Miller invested in R&D at the same time that the company was laying off thousands. Investing in the future was deemed the best way to remain a viable company for a long time to come. As Volkema put it, "We had to do something to make sure some of the folks made it to the other side." Making investments that might not pay off for five years during a deep downturn impressed Clayton Christensen, Harvard Business School professor, and author of *The Innovator's Dilemma.* "Barely one of 1,000 companies would do what they did," Christensen said. "It was a daring bet in terms of increasing spending for the sake of tomorrow while you're cutting back to survive today."

Gary Miller observed that with respect to the team, as with so much of Herman Miller, "the power of the idea prevails." Instead of having an agenda imposed from above, the team "ended up taking assignments basically based upon the area of interest, or area of sort of resonance with all the research issues, from each member. So if somebody would raise their hand and say, 'I'd like to work with this arena,' and the point was go do it." Overall, Miller noted, "it was a scouting model with a high degree of deference to individual's areas of confidence and creative energy. And everybody around the table was chosen, at one level or another, for their already demonstrated ability and proficiency at learning things."

Granted, it took an act by top management of Herman Miller to establish the team in the first place. As Gary Miller noted, though, "the ideas that percolate the business opportunities didn't come from the top down, only the construct and the commission of resources to investigate.... At some level the people around the table, and particularly the extended support around the table at the Creative Office, weren't highly positioned folks. So they're at various levels within the organization.... I think we, the team, would get high grades for a high degree of sort of democracy around the table, where the strength of the idea prevailed... The very nature of the work teams and the interaction that we try to encourage between managers and their staffs, encourages a bottom up sort of set of ideas."

While the upper reaches of the management hierarchy had acted as catalyst for *Purple*, its execution involved the sort of surrender that has defined the company. Upper management surrendered much of the idea generation and design concepts to outside partners. In addition, the internal team creation was grounded in traditional Herman Miller multi-level, multi-functional style. Part of the *Purple* initiative involved creation of an "accessories" team to pursue opportunities with respect to lighting, climate control, and other ancillary aspects of the office which went beyond basic furniture. Robyn Hofmeyer, from finance, created the team. She was given virtual carte blanche in choosing the six-person team, "I'm so amazed how people have been so willing to let very talented people who are playing a very important role in their own organizations, have this opportunity."

   Much of the environment in which the Herman Miller Company operates has changed since D. J. De Pree ran the company. The company he ran was privately held; it had sales of less than $20 million (as opposed to more than $2 billion today), and fewer than 1,000 employees (as opposed to more than 10,000 today). Yet D. J. had the vision of a company that would reach outward for creativity and ideas—something that became the basis for today's Herman Miller. Herman Miller has been blessed, Gary Miller suggested, by leaders who "committed the company in a couple of periods of time away from the constraints of a mature market into a new market. I'd love to see that we're doing that again today." Time will tell.

CHAPTER TAKEAWAYS

1. Values and Culture are central to the highly effective practice of shared leadership at Herman Miller. Notably, an emphasis is placed on everyone contributing, the primacy of ideas and expertise over hierarchy, and the importance of perpetual innovation.
2. Recognizing the extraordinary in everyone and enabling employees to contribute as whole persons underlies the spirit of empowerment that permeates the company. Creating a context for empowered employees sets the stage for sharing leadership across the organization.
3. Shared leadership means that everyone is involved in the leadership process when and where they are most needed. Herman Miller relies on the idea of using "Roving Leaders" to establish this free flowing flexible leadership orientation. According to Max De Pree, leadership "arises and expresses itself at varying times and in varying situations, according to the dictates of those situations. Roving leaders have the special gifts or the special strengths or the special temperament to lead in these special situations."
4. Shared leadership does not occur on its own; rather it is supported by organizational systems, such as sharing in financial rewards. Herman Miller does this with a gainsharing plan, based on a Scanlon Plan and employee stock ownership, which assures that everyone has incentives to perform and participate in the financial success of the company.
5. Sharing the creative process both within and outside the company—independent contracted designers and other stakeholders that reside in the supply chain are embraced as an essential part of Herman Miller's performance network.

CHAPTER 9

W. L. GORE & ASSOCIATES HAS CREATED AN ENTIRE SHARED LEADERSHIP CULTURE

Frank Shipper, Greg L. Stewart, and Charles C. Manz

We have a lot of leaders. In any given day 50 percent of the people are probably leaders and 50 percent are probably followers in one way or another.
—Gore Technical Associate

FUNDAMENTAL CHAPTER THEME

Lead your business without bosses... Instead, create an entire culture of shared leadership.

The story of W. L. Gore and Associates is remarkable. It is the story of a company organized in an unprecedented way with a revolutionary leadership approach that involves everyone in the influence process. Most of all, it is a story of comprehensive, organization-wide shared leadership from top to bottom, inside out, and from one end to the other. Gore eschews

---

Share, Don't Take the Lead, pages 125–145
Copyright © 2014 by Information Age Publishing

traditional hierarchical leadership in favor of a process of shared influence that requires leaders to emerge through informal channels. Leadership status isn't determined by titles and positions but rather through commitments and proactive followership practiced by self-led, team-oriented employees or "associates" as they are called at Gore.

In 2008, W.L. Gore & Associates celebrated its 50th anniversary. Over the five decades, Gore has grown from a start-up operating in founder Bill Gore's basement to a global company widely known for its innovative and quality products. The organization now ranks as one of the largest private companies in the United States with revenues of more than $2.5 billion. Gore was selected as one of the U.S. "100 Best Companies to Work For" in 2009 by *Fortune* magazine for the twelfth consecutive year. In addition, Gore was included in all three *100 Best Companies to Work For in America* books (1984, 1985, and 1993). It is one of only a select few companies to appear on all 15 lists. Gore has also been selected as one of the best companies to work for in Germany, France, Italy, Spain, Sweden, and the United Kingdom.

Much of Gore's success can be traced to its innovative products made from polytetrafluoroethylene, commonly known in the scientific community as PTFE. However, another key to success stems from its unique culture of shared leadership.

TOP LEADERS MODEL A CULTURE
OF SHARED LEADERSHIP

Success in sharing leadership usually begins at the top. The founders and subsequent top-level leaders at Gore have consistently worked to develop a culture that shuns elitism and allows every associate the opportunity to emerge as a leader. Much of the leadership aspects of the culture are summed up by a technical associate who stated, "We have a lot of leaders. In any one day, 50 percent of the people are probably leaders, and 50 percent are followers in one way or the other." An associate may be leading someone on a project one day and then following that same individual on a different project the next day.

The culture emphasizes leadership based on actual contributions rather than formal status. The genesis of this culture is clearly traced to founders Bill and Vieve Gore. Bill was a research scientist working at DuPont who felt that PTFE had ideal insulating properties that could be used to improve electronic equipment. He tried many ways to make a PTFE-coated ribbon cable but with no success until a breakthrough came in his home basement laboratory. One night, while Bill was explaining the problem to his 19-year-old son, Bob, the young Gore saw some PTFE sealant tape and asked his father, "Why don't you try this tape?" Bill explained that everyone knew that you could not bond PTFE to itself. After Bob went to bed, however, Bill remained in the basement lab and proceeded to try what conventional wisdom said could not be done. At about 5:00 am Bill woke up his son, waving a small piece of cable around and saying excitedly, "It works, it works." The following night father and son returned to the basement lab to make ribbon cable insulated with PTFE. Because the idea came from Bob, the patent for the cable was issued in his name. Allowing individuals to emerge as leaders and giving them credit for success has become a hallmark of the Gore culture.

The humble, egalitarian culture where leadership extends beyond position and status was built into the Gore organization from the beginning. The basement of Bill and Vieve Gore's home served as the company's first facility. They officially founded the company on their 23rd wedding anniversary, New Year's Day of 1958. That morning, after breakfast, Vieve turned to her husband of 23 years and said, "Well, let's clear up the dishes, go downstairs, and get to work."

The first few years were rough. Some of the young company's associates lived in the Gore home and accepted Gore stock in lieu of salary. At one point, 11 associates were living and working under one roof. One afternoon, while sifting PTFE powder, Vieve received a call from the City of Denver's water department. The caller wanted to ask some technical questions about the ribbon cable and asked for the product manager. Vieve explained that he was not in at the moment (Bill and two other key associates were out of town.) The caller asked for the sales manager and then for the president. Vieve explained that "they" were also not in. The caller finally shouted, "What kind of a company is this anyway?" With a little diplomacy the Gores were eventually able to secure an order from Denver's water department for around $100,000. This order put the company over the start-up bump and onto profitable footing. Sales began to take off. Yet, even after decades of growth, success has not resulted in greater formalization of specific management roles or jobs at Gore.

In 1986, Bill died while backpacking in the Wind River Mountains of Wyoming.

Ten years earlier Bob had succeeded his father as company president and continued to emphasize a culture of equality among associates. A good illustration of how Bob's actions communicated the company culture came from Dave Gioconda, a current product specialist:

> Two weeks after I joined Gore, I traveled to Phoenix for training . . . I told the guy next to me on the plane where I worked, and he said, "I work for Gore, too." "No kidding?" I asked. "Where do you work?" He said, "Oh, I work over at the Cherry Hill plant." . . .

I spent two and a half hours on this plane having a conversation with this gentleman who described himself as a technologist and shared some of his experiences. As I got out of the plane, I shook his hand and said, "I'm Dave Gioconda, nice to meet you." He replied, "Oh, I'm Bob Gore." That experience has had a profound influence on the decisions that I make.

This emphasis on informality and collaboration continues, with many current employees describing the culture as "tribal." It is a culture where looking out for oneself at the expense of others is unwelcome. As one current associate put it, "if you have a big ego here, I don't think you are going to do well." Or as another associate said, "you can be really great but really egocentric, and basically, people will just ignore you."

In 2000, Chuck Carroll became the third president of Gore, and in 2005, Terri Kelly became the current president. Terri, who also serves as CEO, was with Gore for 22 years before assuming her current role. A good example of how Terri continues to live the values espoused in the Gore culture comes from a recent experience overseas. Given the need to protect its proprietary knowledge, Gore associates are encouraged to closely guard technical information and only share it on a need-to-know basis. As Terri was visiting a facility in Shenzhen, China she became curious about a new laminate that was being commercialized. She asked a number of technical questions, but the development engineer kept dodging her questions. Finally he smiled, and said, "Now Terri, do you have a need to know?"

As Terri retells the incident, "He played back exactly what he was supposed to, which is don't share with someone, even if it's a CEO, something that they have no need to know." She laughed and said, "You're right. I'm just being nosy."

Terri continued, "And everyone's—I could see the look in their eyes—thinking, 'Is he going to get fired?' He had taken a great personal risk, certainly for someone in that local culture. We laughed, and we joked and for the next week, it became the running joke."

The actions and examples of top leaders have thus been, and continue to be, an important key for creating and communicating a culture that facilitates comprehensive shared leadership at Gore. From the very beginning top-level leaders have downplayed status differences. For any given activity the person with the most relevant knowledge and skill is seen as the most capable leader. Every associate at Gore is seen as capable of leadership. As Terri Kelly puts it, "A lot of what our culture values is not about the leaders and being empowered, it's about empowering others."

For another striking example of shared leadership, in another culture, see Box 9.1 about leadership at Yuhan Kimberly. CEO Moon's leadership behavior provides a powerful model of prioritizing mutual respect and collaboration over status.

BOX 9.1—DE-EMPHASIZING STATUS TO DEVELOP SHARED LEADERSHIP AT YUHAN-KIMBERLY IN KOREA

Craig L. Pearce and Young-Chul Chang

Upon becoming CEO of Yuhan-Kimbery, Mr. Moon, Kook Hyun found himself confronted with a strike... and not just any ordinary strike. The senior leaders of the union commandeered and occupied his office: They staged a good old fashioned sit-in. Mr. Moon's advisors strongly counseled him to avoid the office and to let the authorities handle the situation. He did not heed their advice. To the contrary, he entered the office humbly, knelt down, crossed his legs, and joined the sit-in. This was an unconventional and unprecedented action, especially in the Korean context, where probity of position is paramount. He proceeded to engage those present in a dialogue that was just the start of an amazing journey for Yuhan-Kimberly, and its entire workforce.

This unconventional approach was but the first in a series of actions he took to de-emphasize status differences and power differentials. In fact, the organizational lure is filled to the brim with stories about how Mr. Moon systematically, brick by brick, built an organizational culture founded on shared leadership. Yuhan-Kimberly is a phenomenal success story—they dominate the Korean paper products industry. But their story has more texture to it than that. They have engendered a sense of purpose that transcends the myopic bottom line of modern day business practice: They believe in proactively impacting their social milieu and their physical environment. For example, they created a paid staff to help the government of Korea translate Yuhan-Kimberly's phenomenal productivity into other sectors of the economy, free of charge. Moreover, they created a re-forestation program, even thought there was no compelling business reason or governmental compliance stipulation. These are but a couple of the organizational causes around which the workforce rallies and acts in unison; pulling together to enhance each others' lives.

The moral of the story of Mr. Moon and Yuhan-Kimberly is that de-emphasizing status differences and power differentials and focusing on what each of us can contribute unleashes amazing human potential. Yuhan-Kimberly show how the applicability of shared leadership transcends national boarders and cultural boundaries.

THE ORGANIZATIONAL STRUCTURE IS EMERGENT AND FLEXIBLE

The egalitarian culture of comprehensive shared leadership is supported by a revolutionary organizational structure. The structure may be the world's shortest organizational pyramid for a company of its size. Gore is a company largely without titles, hierarchical organization charts, or any other conventional structural arrangement typically employed by enterprises with billions of dollars in sales revenues and thousands of employees.

For product management, Gore is divided into four divisions—electronics, fabrics, industrial, and medical. The electronic products division develops and manufactures high-performance cables and assemblies as well as specialty materials for electronic devices. The fabrics division develops and provides fabric to the outdoor clothing industry as well as the military, law enforcement, and fire protection industries. Gore fabrics marketed under the GORE-TEX®, WINDSTOPPER®, CROSSTECH®, and GORE® CHEMPAK® labels provide the wearer protection while remaining comfortable. The industrial products division makes filtration, sealant and other products. These products meet diverse contamination and process challenges in many industries. The Gore medical division provides products such as synthetic vascular grafts, interventional devices, endovascular stent-grafts, surgical meshes for hernia repair, and sutures for use in vascular, cardiac, general surgery and oral procedures.

Although the divisions are relatively independent, in Gore's collaborative environment, associates from different areas can work together easily in teams that span different areas of the organization. Effective leaders actively coordinate across the divisions and teams. As one leader explained:

> People who are really effective in this organization are able to prevent breakdowns at cross-functional boundaries, at interfaces between different teams and different groups. They're able to build the teamwork across those boundaries, network and collaborate well and make good decisions and draw on the right people. That is when the system really works well, and then everybody is energized and engaged and not being told to do something. They're excited about doing it because somebody has helped manage the conflicting needs of different groups and teams.

Even though there are multiple divisions, the positions with formal titles presented to the public are few. Instead of individual leaders with corporate titles, references are made frequently to the ELT, or Enterprise Leadership Team, a four-person, cross-functional group responsible for the overall health and growth of Gore. The ELT meets monthly to consider issues having enterprise-wide reach and impact. The participative actions of members of the team combined with the lack of hierarchical structure result in a perception of shared leadership where the ELT is empowering rather than domineering. Rather than a hierarchical structure, Gore emphasizes shared leadership through the use of its unique lattice structure (See Figure 9.1). The features of Gore's lattice structure include the following:

1. Direct lines of communication—person to person—with no intermediary
2. No fixed or assigned authority
3. Sponsors, not bosses
4. Natural leadership as evidenced by the willingness of others to follow
5. Objectives set by those who must "make them happen"
6. Tasks and functions organized through commitments

According to Bill Gore, "Every successful organization has an underground lattice. It's where the news spreads like lightning, where people can go around the organization to get things done." The lattice structure, as described by the people at Gore, is more similar to this informal network than it is to the formal, hierarchical structures found in most large organizations. The lattice is complex and depends on interpersonal interactions, self-commitment to group-known responsibilities, natural leadership, and group-imposed discipline.

Because there is no chain of command or assigned authority within the lattice structure, some wonder how this system affects the decision-making process. Could it lead to slower response times and less decisive action? Gore associates say that hesitancy and indecision are not characteristics of the enterprise. They distinguish between two types of decisions. First, for time-critical decisions, they maintain that the lattice structure is faster in response than traditional structures because you are not hampered by

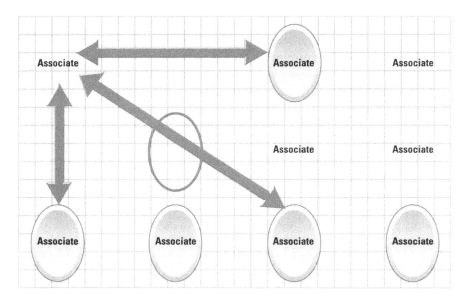

Figure 9.1   Gore's lattice structure.

bureaucracy. The leader who has responsibility assembles a knowledge-based team to examine and resolve the issue. The team members can be recruited by the leader from any area of the company if their expertise is needed. Once the issue is resolved, the team ceases to exist, and its members return to their respective areas. Bob Winterling, a financial associate, asserted, "We have no trouble making crisis decisions, and we do it very swiftly and very quickly."

The other type of decision relates to critical issues that will have a significant impact on the enterprise's long-term operations. Associates admit that such decisions can sometimes take a little longer than they would like. Chrissy Lyness, another financial associate, stated:

> We get the buy-in up front instead of creating and implementing the solution and putting something out there that doesn't work for everybody. That can be frustrating to new associates, because they're used to a few people putting their heads together, saying, "This is what we're going to do. This is a solution." That's not the way it works at Gore.

> Here, you spend a lot of time at the beginning of the decision-making process gaining feedback, so that when you come out of that process, you have something that's going to work, and the implementation is actually pretty easy.

The associates at Gore believe that time spent in the beginning tapping into the best ideas and gaining consensus pays off in the implementation. They believe that authoritarian decision making may save time initially, but the quality of the decision and translating it into action will not be as good as a decision made by consensus. In addition, they believe that authoritarian decisions will take longer to implement than those made by consensus.

Given the lack of formal structure, associates face some interesting obstacles when they join Gore. Rather than being confined to a specific role, they are expected to form a set of commitments that define their contribution. Brad Jones, a member of the Enterprise Leadership Team, described his experience of joining Gore after a number of years working for DuPont:

> It was a story of, "Here's a desk, here's a phone, here's an officemate. Kind of wander around and get to know the business and the microfiltration group," which is where I started. "And find some stuff to do, and we'll talk about it.

> And I ended up inheriting a lot of the troubled projects that, you know, had reached a brick wall for one reason or another. But what was really going on was people were getting to know me. And over time, a line started to form outside my door. Eventually I was leading the microfiltration group. And over time, I began to emerge as leader of the industrial products division.

The lack of structure can be daunting for some new associates, but over a period of a few months most are able to establish a set of commitments that play to their individual strengths. The informal structure can also be very helpful for enabling shared leadership to adapt and respond to changing business demands. An interesting example came from Chrissy Lyness' description of what occurred as Gore began producing and selling GLIDE® Floss, a brand of dental floss, in the early 1990s:

> Have you ever seen the commercial, and it's years old—where there's a group of people sitting around a computer screen, and they get some orders. And they're like, "Yeah!" And they get a bunch more orders, and they're like, "Yeah!" And then they get a whole slew of orders, and its like, "Oh, no."
>
> Well, that's kind of what GLIDE® Floss was. We were not anticipating the demand as quickly as it happened. So we had our operations leader in our plant processing credit cards. We had our HR people and our accountants out on the floor packaging GLIDE® Floss. We had everybody in that facility pitch in to make sure that we got GLIDE® Floss out the door. It didn't matter what your role was. It didn't matter what you did.
>
> We did everything we could. We had to make decisions on the fly. We had a business leader for GLIDE® Floss come into our accounting office and say, "We need to find a way to process credit card orders." And we said, "Okay, we'll call the bank. How long do we have?" And he said, "We started taking orders last week."
>
> So, it was just that kind of atmosphere where it didn't matter what your role was—you just pitched in to do what you had to do to get this product off the ground. And it became one of our most profitable and well-known products.

What would have taken months to accomplish in a lot of other organizations occurred almost instantly in Gore's flexible lattice structure with shared leadership. Interestingly, the lattice structure also helped smooth the transition when the GLIDE® Floss brand was sold to Procter & Gamble. Gore still provides the fiber to Procter & Gamble, but the sale of the brand initially displaced a number of people in the GLIDE® Floss team. All of them were absorbed into other areas of the operation that allowed them to establish new sets of commitments that defined their contributions in a new way.

The lattice structure thus allows leaders to emerge in areas where they have unique knowledge and skills. Normally rigid roles and formal relationships are replaced with emerging commitments. Gore's leaders believe that the company's unique organization structure has proven to be a significant contributor to associate satisfaction and retention. Gore reports a low voluntary turnover rate for all its associates in all stages of their careers. *Fortune* magazine reports a turnover rate of 5% for Gore. In addition, it reports

19,108 applicants for 276 new jobs in 2008. In other words, it is harder to get a job at Gore than to get accepted into a very elite university.

STRONG SOCIAL RELATIONSHIPS CREATE CRITICAL LINKS

In order for the lattice structure and the corresponding practice of shared leadership to work, associates need to build and maintain strong social relationships. Donna Frey, a member of the Enterprise Leadership Team and leader of the Human Resources team, suggests that the one-on-one relationship is really the foundation of how people work together. To be successful, an associate needs to know something about the knowledge and skills of other associates. It is also important to have connections that enable associates to establish emergent ties that facilitate cooperation. This process of building social ties begins as soon as an associate joins Gore. As Donna Frey explains:

> When new associates join the enterprise, they participate in an orientation program. Then, each new associate works with a starting sponsor to get acclimated and begin building relationships within Gore. The starting sponsor provides the new hire with a list of key associates he/she should meet with during the next few months.
>
> We encourage the new hire to meet with these associates one-on-one. It's not a phone conversation, but a chance to sit down with them face-to-face and get to know them.
>
> This process helps demonstrate the importance of relationships. When you're hiring really good people, they want to have quick wins and make contributions, and building relationships without a clear goal can be difficult. Often, new associates will say, "I don't feel like I'm contributing. I've spent three months just getting to know people." However, after a year they begin to realize how important this process was.

The emphasis on face-to-face communication is critical. Of course, Gore associates use E-mail, especially to send attachments. In many cases, associates also use Gorecom, which is a company-specific voicemail system. According to Terri Kelly, "Gorecom is the preferred media if you want a quick response." However, to foster the oral-based shared leadership culture, associates are expected to meet face-to-face, regularly. As one sales leader puts it, "It's hard to do on the phone and email . . . We have scheduled conference calls and video conferencing, but I can't get close to recreating the face-to-face that you have when you go to build those relationships. You go with the people and spend time there and it's part of how you work."

To meet the need for face-to-face interaction, Gore spends a lot of time and money getting people from different functions and geographical locations together. The goal is to make people aware of what is happening in different corners of the organization, and to help people know who the thought leaders and experts are in different areas. Of course, this is increasingly difficult in today's global business environment. According to CEO Terri Kelly,

> In the early days, our business was largely conducted at the local level. There were global operations, but most relationships were built regionally, and most decisions were made regionally. That picture has evolved dramatically over the last 20 years, as businesses can no longer be defined by brick and mortar. Today, most of our teams are spread across regions and continents. Therefore, the decision-making process is much more global and virtual in nature, and there's a growing need to build strong relationships across geographical boundaries. The globalization of our business has been one of the biggest changes I've seen in the last 25 years.

For team members and especially leaders, meeting face-to-face means lots of travel. As one technical associate joked, "Probably, in the last 12 years, I spent three years internationally, a couple of weeks at a time."

Relationships created through close social interactions become an important mechanism for influencing others and getting things done through shared leadership. Ray Davis, a manufacturing leader, acknowledges that he gets most of his energy by dealing with people, and working with others to solve problems. He says, "I don't necessarily need a bunch of spreadsheets, or paper, or organizational skills to be successful. As long as you have the connections and relationships with folks, it's easy at Gore to get things done, and to leverage other peoples' strengths in order to get things done. His sentiment is echoed by another manufacturing leader, Richard Buckingham:

> So much of it is interaction with others. Certainly, we do look at delivery-on-time reports, inventory reports, and all those kinds of things as manufacturing leaders. Of course. But to say you're buried in that every day? You could be, if you chose to be. But I can influence many more things indirectly with other people, kind of guide the organization, as opposed to having my nose buried in a computer every day.
>
> Because of the relationships that I have with different people, I can influence their thinking to some degree, and the direction they're going, or maybe have some insight about where the business is going that causes them to go, "Oh, if that's the case, then I need to commit to this."

Rather than doing things themselves, effective leaders at Gore practice shared leadership, relying on strong relationships to leverage the knowledge and skills of others. As one technical leader puts it, "our job does become less technical and more like a team psychologist. Interaction is the key. It's like you're hiring a lot of people who are—I'll speak for myself—way smarter than I am and have abilities way beyond anything I can do. You're just trying to help them to work well together and to have enough access." One analogy used to describe the leadership role is a snowplow that removes obstacles for others. Leaders are more enablers than directors.

The team oriented nature of leadership combined with a belief in the importance of the individual heightens the importance of good social relationships. The idea of managers controlling employees is replaced by a sense of camaraderie and shared responsibility. The perspective of shared responsibility means that Gore associates often go above and beyond for each other, whether facing business challenges or in times of personal crisis. For example, one associate based in Delaware was on business in Scotland when she received a call that her mother had been hospitalized. The following is how she related what happened next:

> I flew home and I went straight to Pittsburgh to be with my mother. I had my computer with me, and I connected to the wireless internet at the hospital. I sent e-mails to my team saying, "Hey, guys, I'm out in Pittsburgh," and they replied, "What are you doing on email? Take care of your mom. Why are you even worrying about this?" And that's really what it's all about.

Social relationships become a mechanism for bonding employees together. Activities at Gore are coordinated by emergent relationships within the lattice structure that replace hierarchical status and formal lines of authority. The power to influence comes not from positions and titles but rather from strong social ties that create a sense of mutual respect.

PEOPLE FOLLOW CREDIBLE LEADERS

Within Gore, leaders are often defined by 'followership.' This is because leaders emerge when they gain credibility with other associates. Gore refers to this process as "natural leadership." Credibility is gained by demonstrating special knowledge, skill, or experience that advances a business objective, a series of successes, and involving others in significant decisions. Those associates who do these three things find that other associates naturally follow them. As a technical specialist said, "Credibility is currency in our culture.... people with a track record get more latitude." This concept is further explained by financial specialist Bob Winterling:

Don't think for a second that credibility doesn't have a lot to do with things. So how do you get it? I mean, how do you build those trust deposits in the bank, so to speak, that you can tap into every once in a while and pull the deposits out every once in a while? How do you do that? Well, at Gore it's pretty brutal. I mean, it doesn't happen because I have an MBA and I've come from a great company by walking through the doors. No, you have to build it everyday.

Shared leadership built on credibility is a fluid process at Gore. Associates step forward to lead when they have the expertise to do so. This practice is referred to as *knowledge-based decision-making*. Based on this practice decisions are "…made by the most knowledgeable person, not the person in charge," according to Terri Kelly. The company's preference for knowledge-based decision making is illustrated by the actions of Bob Gore. As one associate explains, "I used to say that interaction with Bob Gore was interesting because he would respect logic and facts and data. That was a nice thing because no matter if you were just out of school or you were a 20-year PhD, it was, 'Whose argument held water better?' It wasn't a natural predisposition to, 'That guy's right, and that guy's wrong.' And that's what I think was really empowering."

Knowledge-based decision making also flows naturally from the four guiding principles established by Bill Gore:

1. Associates should try to be fair with each other, suppliers, customers, and all persons with whom they conduct business.
2. Associates should encourage, help, and allow other associates to grow in knowledge, skill, and scope of activity and responsibility. This is in line with the belief that associates will more than exceed expectations when given the freedom and encouragement to do so.
3. Associates should make their own commitments and keep them. Unlike commands, which produce obedience at best, commitments call upon the total energies, talents and dedication of the persons making them.
4. Associates should consult with other associates before taking actions that may be "below the waterline" and cause serious damage to the enterprise.

The four principles are referred to as *fairness, freedom, commitment,* and *waterline.* The waterline principle is drawn from an analogy to ships. If someone pokes a hole in a boat above the waterline, the boat will be in relatively little real danger. If, however, someone pokes a hole below the waterline, the boat is in immediate danger of sinking. The expectation is that decisions that are considered important enough to be "waterline" issues will be discussed across teams, plants, and continents before those decisions are made. This principle is still emphasized even though team members who need to share in the decision making process are now spread across the globe.

Building credibility by following the guiding principles provides an environment where anyone who is a high performer can emerge to exert influence as part of the shared leadership process. One example is Rich Buckingham who started as a maintenance mechanic 30 years ago and has now progressed to become a manufacturing leader in the fabrics division. He described his path by saying, "I was fortunate enough to have many sponsors over the years that would tend to see some little spark of something in me, and say, 'Gosh, the business is going this direction. You might want to think about looking at that.' In most instances, I listened, and here I am today." In a similar way, Susan Bartley, a manufacturing leader with 17 years experience, pointed out that what she actually does has nothing to do with her education or college degree. Over the years she did what she was good at doing, which helped her succeed in a career very different from what she envisioned when she first joined the company.

A good example of knowledge-based decision making and shared leadership is Gore's experience with a product called GORE™ RIDE ON® Bike Cables. Initially, they were derailleur and brake cables for trail bikes. They were developed by some trail bike enthusiasts at the medical facilities in Flagstaff, Arizona in the 1990s. When the trail bike market declined, the product was withdrawn from the market. In 2006, a group of young engineers went to Jack Kramer, a technical leader and member of the Enterprise Leadership Team, and said that they wanted to learn what it takes to develop a new product by reviving GORE™ RIDE ON® Bike Cables. His response was, "You need someone who has some experience before you go off and try to do that."

One of the young engineers approached Lois Mabon, a product specialist who had about 16 years of experience at Gore and worked in the same facility, and asked her to be the group's coach. Lois went back to Jack and talked to him. He was still not sold on the idea, but he allowed Lois to find out what had happened to the bike cables and explore with the group what it would take to bring a new product to market. Within Gore, associates are encouraged to set aside some *dabble* time. Dabble time is when people have the freedom to develop new products and evaluate their viability. After some exploration of what happened to the cables, Lois led a group that made a presentation to Jack and some others in the company, and even though they still were not sure if the product should be revived, they said, "All right, keep working on it."

After nine or ten months of exploring the possibility and developing a team of excited and passionate associates, ideas were developed for a set of GORE™ RIDE ON® products. In their exploration, the team learned that the road bike market is larger than the trail bike market and that there might potentially be a product for the racing market.

A presentation, referred to within Gore as a "Real-Win-Worth", was pre-pared. This presentation was made to the leadership team of the industrial products division (IPD). The three issues that must be addressed in this presentation are

1. Is the idea real?
2. Can Gore win in the market
3. Is it worth pursuing?

After listening and questioning the presenters, the IPD leadership team responded, "You know what? You do have some really good ideas. Let's do a market study on it. Let's see if the market is interested in GORE™ RIDE ON® Bike Cables."

Some samples of the new product were made and taken to the top 200 bike stores across the United States. They were handed out to the store owners, and in turn, the store owners were asked to fill out a survey. Based on these results the team concluded that people would really want to buy the product.

So with that data in hand, another presentation was made to the IPD leadership team in August 2006. The response was, "Okay, go launch it." The product team had 12 months to improve the mountain bike cables, develop the new road bike cables, redesign the packaging, redesign the logo, set up production and do everything else that is associated with a new product introduction.

Every division in Gore was involved in producing and launching the prod-uct. The product was overseen by a team in the industrial products division. The GORE BIKE WEAR® products team in the fabrics division served as the sales team. The medical products division made a component that went into the cables. And the electronics products division coated the cables.

As illustrated by this story, sharing and enhancing knowledge is the key. According to Terri Kelly, "There's a real willingness and openness to share knowledge. That's something I experienced 25 years ago, and it's not changed today. This is a healthy thing. We want to make sure folks under-stand the need to connect more dots in the lattice."

Associates build credibility by sharing technical knowledge, especially among the engineers and other scientists. For example, a core leader-ship team consisting of eight technical associates gets together every other month and reviews each other's plans and tries to make connections. Ac-cording to Jack Kramer, "We put a lot of effort into trying to make sure that we connect informally and formally across a lot of these boundaries." One way associates connect formally to share knowledge is through monthly technical meetings, where scientists and engineers from different divisions present information to other associates and colleagues. These presentations are described by others in attendance as passionate and exciting.

Failure to work together and share leadership decreases credibility and is unacceptable. For example, one product specialist related the following instance:

> There was this guy on my team that I had to part ways with last month. Really, what it came down to is he wanted to sit in an office with a spreadsheet and look and say, "Oh, operations' contract is too high this month. Let's get on the phone and call the operations guy and get that fixed." He wanted to do that as opposed to say, "Okay. Let's go figure out why operations isn't working well and why we can't get the orders out on time, and why we're not getting the booking orders we expected."

As the example illustrates, W.L. Gore & Associates isn't the right place for everyone to work; people who don't contribute in a cooperative way find the environment rather uncomfortable. In place of traditional reporting relationships, associates are held accountable by their peers. This process is explained by a technical leader:

> I would say the funny thing about accountability is—and maybe this is a debatable point—but for me, the greatest accountability really comes from peer pressure and not managerial pressure. I don't see business leaders coming down on people or people getting called into the office. What I see is people generally aware of what you're doing because we have a lot of forums, especially in the technical function, focused on what we're doing.

> People can tell immediately whether or not they're doing what's valued or not by the amount of respect that they generate with others. And it becomes apparent if you're not really producing and doing stuff that's valuable.

A major part of the success story at Gore thus focuses on allowing associates the freedom to follow credible leaders. This helps assure that leadership is shared and the people with critical knowledge are involved in critical decisions. Successful leaders build credibility by involving and empowering others. This path to emerging as a leader is summarized by financial leader Chrissy Lyness who says, "Gaining credibility is a matter of successes along the way and making sure that you get the right people involved in decisions. You make sure that when you're trying to influence something that you have your ducks in a row—you have all the facts, and you and your team have investigated the pros and the cons and feel pretty strongly about the solution."

HR PRACTICES ALIGN AND SUPPORT

The culture and informal structure at Gore are supported by a variety of human resources practices that align with and facilitate shared leadership. An emphasis on cooperation and social skills begins during recruiting and hiring where great care is taken to identify and select individuals who fit with the collaborative Gore culture. Brad Jones of the ELT described the process by noting that " . . . when we hire someone we're not just looking at grades on a transcript or a list of specific accomplishments on a resume. We're absolutely, explicitly looking for cultural compatibility. Is this the sort of person that I can deal with? Is this someone I want on my team? It's very important to Gore."

Since Gore receives a large number of applications for each position, new associates are carefully selected. The selection process begins with a resume review and screening interview. Each candidate who passes the initial screening is interviewed by a group of associates from the team in which the person is expected to start working. The applicant is interviewed one-on-one by a number of different associates and leaders. A manufacturing leader described the process and characteristics being sought in applicants:

> Well, there will be a team interviewing any candidate. It doesn't matter if we're talking to the housekeeper or divisional leader. That team will meet to try to come up with some kind of criteria. What are we looking for? Are we all on the same page with what we're looking for around this commitment?
>
> But besides the kind of core skills that may be needed around a specific commitment, we're looking for good communication skills, looking for some kind of ability to resolve conflicts on your own . . . it really doesn't matter what the role is. . . . Just in general, how collaborative do they tend to be?
>
> Many times, you interview and find someone is overly competitive. We all get competitive at times. That's not a bad thing, but it can be. So someone who is overly competitive, or overly focused on me, me, me, isn't going to fit here very well. So you try and sort those things out, see how they'll fit with our culture, and the way we want to interact, and who we want to be.

When it comes to leadership, Terri Kelly summarized the type of person Gore looks for in new recruits this way: an associate as "self-directed" and a leader as grasping "the idea of not being in charge that your job is to help empower the team." Command and control leaders are not effective at Gore.

Before someone can be hired, a current associate must step forward and make a commitment to be the applicant's sponsor. The sponsor's role is to take a personal interest in the new associate's contributions, problems, and goals, acting as both a coach and an advocate. The sponsor tracks the new associate's progress, offers help and encouragement, points out weaknesses and suggests ways to correct them, and concentrates on how the associate can better make use of his or her strengths. Sponsoring is not a short-term commitment. All associates have sponsors, and many have more than one. When individuals are hired initially, they are likely to have a sponsor in their immediate work area. As associates' commitments change or grow, it is normal for them to acquire additional sponsors. For instance, if they move to a new job in another area of the company, they will typically gain a sponsor there.

To ensure that new associates are not overwhelmed by what may be their first experience in a non-hierarchical organization, Gore has an orientation program it calls Building on the Best. New associates are brought together with other new associates after two or three months. In this program they discuss with their sponsors and other leaders "...who we are as an enterprise and the experiences they've had. How can we try to help them as they've begun to hit a few walls, and how do you get through and over those walls and frustrations that you have coming into a less structured organization?" according to Donna Frey.

Continual learning is encouraged through other formal training programs, many of which teach technical skills. However, substantial development, particularly in the area of leadership, is done through mentoring and coaching. Donna Frey described this effort:

> One of the things that we've begun to really focus on is that we have to better prepare our current leaders on how to develop future leaders, and I think that is all about coaching. We know that 85 to 90 percent of the development will come from there. The rest of it will come from more formal kinds of learning. But the coaching part of that is extremely important.

Another human resources practice that facilitates cooperation, teamwork and shared leadership is a team-based performance appraisal. Each associate's contribution is measured by peer evaluations. This process reduces political posturing and allows groups of associates to share in performing the important leadership function of evaluation. Brad Jones of the ELT highlights his attraction to the idea of peer evaluations. "I liked the idea of an organization where people are recognized based on the team's assessment of their performance as opposed to it all depending on how well you've pulled the wool over one individual boss's eyes."

The specific type of peer performance appraisal is unique in that it is neither a typical measure of individual contribution nor a group-level measure of accomplishment. The measure acknowledges individual contribution but only in the context of how that contribution serves the good of the larger group. The motivational pull of this emphasis on individual contribution to the group was captured by the words of a product specialist:

> But here at Gore, we have this interesting paradox, which is we're all in it together. It's a sense of what we are trying to achieve together, yet we have this system of ranking and individual contribution. So you're constantly balancing, "Hey, I need to make my individual contribution," but it's usually best received in the sense that your contribution is bettering the whole. You're able to be more successful if the team has success than if you have individual success. Somehow, that's embedded in all of us.

The peer performance evaluation results feed directly into compensation. Changes in annual compensation are linked to peer rankings. Gore also uses profit sharing to encourage cooperation and contribution to the larger enterprise. Profit shares, which are calculated as a percentage of annual salary, are distributed when established financial goals are reached. Every month the business results are reviewed with associates, and they know whether they are on track to meet forecasts.

Beyond short-term equity sharing, Gore establishes long-term commitment through an associates' stock ownership program (ASOP).[1] Each year Gore contributes up to 12% of pay to an account that purchases Gore stock for associates with more than one year of service. Associates have ownership of the account after three years of service, when they become 100% vested. Gore also has a 401(K) Plan. It provides a contribution of up to 3% of pay to each associate's personal investment accounts. Associates are eligible after one month of service. Associates are 100% vested immediately.

An interesting compensation practice that fits with the Gore culture but differentiates the organization from others is a lack of sales commissions. Sales representatives receive stock in the ASOP and profit sharing the same as other associates. When a sales associate was asked to explain this practice, he responded as follows:

> The people who are just concerned with making their sales numbers in other companies usually struggle when they come to Gore. We encourage folks to help others. For example, when we hire new sales associates, we ask experienced sales associates to take some time to help get them acclimated to Gore and how we do things. In other companies where I've worked, that would have been seen as something that would detract from your potential to make your number, so you probably wouldn't be asked to do such a thing.

Of course, not everyone stays with Gore for an entire career. Turnover is generally low, but it is higher in the first couple of years. Some people just don't fit. Interestingly, even the process of identifying and separating low performers fits with the culture of shared leadership. A manufacturing leader suggested, "It ends up being a very organic sort of rejection process. I hate to put it in the negative sense, but if someone's just not wired or chooses not to behave in a way that is culturally consistent, then word gets around. Again, very tribal. It's a lot about one-on-one interactions." As another manufacturing associate described it, "It may not always happen like it would in a traditional setting, where somebody in an official position is first going to go, 'You're not working out. You might want to think about going someplace else.' Some associates start to look around and go, 'I'm not working out. I might want to think about going somewhere else.'"

Gore is indeed a unique organization where not everyone feels comfortable working. Thus, great efforts are made to select and integrate associates who are able to work effectively in an egalitarian culture without a formal structure where shared leadership is widely practiced. Emphasis is placed on identifying new associates who can develop social relationships and establish credibility as leaders. Training, evaluation, and compensation practices support the process of shared leadership once associates are onboard.

CHAPTER TAKEAWAYS

1. Top-level leaders at Gore differ from most traditional bosses and managers. They hold no assumed authority, and their public actions display an effective model of empowering others and sharing leadership.

2. Traditional structures with formal roles and hierarchical relationships often inhibit shared leadership. Gore is organized using a lattice structure that promotes shared leadership by emphasizing informal ties and emergent relationships.

3. Shared leadership can sometimes seem inefficient, but the long-term payoff is greater effectiveness. Major decisions at Gore start with seeking a great deal of buy-in and input. Implementation of decisions is usually quick because key people are already onboard.

4. Face-to-face interaction is critical for establishing social relationships. At Gore social relationships are the key to effectively influencing others and sharing leadership.

5. Knowledge-based decision making encourages leadership sharing by assuring that facts and data trump status. Within Gore, decisions are made by the people who have the most knowledge and skill regardless of position.

6. Shared leadership helps assure that the best contributors emerge as leaders regardless of formal education or background. At Gore, associates gain followers when they earn credibility as a leader; that comes from making critical performance contributions.

7. Human resource practices can help facilitate shared leadership. Gore carefully selects associates who have the characteristics that fit its egalitarian culture. Peer evaluation and performance-

based compensation also help facilitate a spirit of shared leadership that contributes to the greater whole.

NOTE

1. Gore's ASOP is similar legally to an employee stock ownership plan (ESOP). Again, Gore simply has never allowed the word *employee* in any of its documentation. The ASOP and profit sharing will be explained in more detail later.

CHAPTER 10

SHARED LEADERSHIP IN A HIGH GROWTH ENVIRONMENT

Realizing the American Dream at Panda Restaurant Group

Michelle C. Bligh and Craig L. Pearce

Deliver Exceptional Asian Dining Experiences
Where People are Inspired to Better Their Lives
—Panda Mission Statement

FUNDAMENTAL CHAPTER THEME

Culture is the only long term source of strategic competitive advantage.

The story of the Panda Restaurant Group—owner of the famous Panda Express Restaurant Chain—combines entrepreneurship, innovation, and profound success in a modern enactment of the American Dream.

Share, Don't Take the Lead, pages 147–162
Copyright © 2014 by Information Age Publishing
All rights of reproduction in any form reserved.

Fundamentally, Panda is an organization that has embraced a model of shared leadership and a culture of inclusiveness throughout a period of dramatic growth. Panda just celebrated their 40th anniversary. Founders Andrew and his father, esecutive chef Ming-Tsai Cherng opened the first restaurant in Pasadena, California in 1973, Panda Inn, which was a full service gourmet Chinese restaurant. Since the founding of the company, they have modestly increased the number of Panda Inns and experimented with multiple different restaurant concepts. In 1983, however, they opened the first Panda Express and it has become the juggernaut that has grown to 1,600 locations today and they have aggressive plans for continued national and international expansion. Panda currently employs over 23,000 Americans, many of whom are Chinese immigrants, reflecting the ongoing legacy of the founders' own experience. Andrew Cherng, who was born in China, came to America to study in mid-1960s. Similarly, Peggy Cherng, who was born in Burma, emigrated to America in the mid-1960s in order to attend college. Andrew and Peggy met in college. Andrew went on to earn a Master's Degree and Peggy earned her PhD and then they opened their first restaurant. Andrew Cherng's original goal was "to survive and to have a place that we could all have a job." But Panda quickly became more than a job, and Panda has grown rapidly into an American restaurant empire.

The Cherngs opened the first Panda Express storefront restaurant at a shopping mall in 1983. From the beginning, they began to revolutionize the concept of the food court restaurant. Today the Panda Restaurant Group has more than 1,600 restaurants with nearly two billion dollars in annual sales, including more than 44 million pounds of orange chicken each year. According to Peggy Cherng, "the most important thing for any business is to really serve your customer well. So at Panda, our philosophy is always focus on great food, great service and great ambiance at each location, and that coupled with great pricing." Panda Express is so successful in the area of customer satisfaction that it often draws additional food service and retail clients to locations, giving it anchor tenant status with landlords that continues to contribute to its rapid growth and success.

Andrew Cherng's entrepreneurial spirit proved to be an excellent fit for American culture. He quickly realized that "in this country, they seem to be much more adaptable to new ideas, new cuisines and new tastes." He capitalized on this openness to new culinary tastes to aggressively expand Panda's menu and customer base. Now U.S. citizens, Andrew and Peggy Cherng run the company together, modeling the idea that leadership is shared even at the top of the organization. The success of Panda Express is due in part to the founder's desire to be involved in the day to day operations of Panda, and both Andrew and Peggy remain very active in running the organization's strategic approach and daily operations. As Andrew himself proclaims, "Yes, I am living the American dream. It is beyond my wildest dream."

A CULTURE OF SHARED LEADERSHIP: SHAPING PANDA'S MISSION AND VALUES

The mission of the Panda Restaurant Group is to deliver exceptional Asian dining experiences by building an organization "where people are inspired to better their lives." This mission is embodied in every aspect of Panda, and the Panda values are infused in nearly everything that the company does. The story of how a company focused on selling Chinese quick service food has transformed itself into an organization focused on developing people is even more remarkable given the intense growth that the company has experienced throughout its short history. In part, this story exemplifies how shared leadership has helped instill a values-based culture in an industry that is known more for employee turnover than transforming employee lives.

The emphasis placed on shared leadership is highly visible throughout the Panda organization. For example, in contrast to more traditional structures with a corporate 'Headquarters' at the top of a hierarchical organization, Panda's Senior Team is located in a "Support Center" that symbolizes its dedication to helping to implement the daily operations of the business. The job of everyone in the support center is to service both operations and the people that form the talent base of the organization, the employees. Panda "invests in our people because great people run great operations that will exceed our guests' expectations." Talking to any of one of Panda's 'associates,' it is clear that Panda's culture is dedicated to its mission and five fundamental values— Proactive, Respect/Win-Win, Growth, Great Operations, and Giving. These values have been consciously instilled throughout the culture of the organization through shared leadership principles that emanate from the top of the organization down to the newest employee. Andrew Cherng was the original CEO of the company. Later Peggy Cherng became the CEO. Then, from 2005 to 2010 Tom Davin, from Taco Bell, become the CEO. Now Andrew and Peggy Cherng are the Co-CEOs—sharing the lead of Panda Restaurant Group. See Box 10.1.

BOX 10.1—PANDA VALUES

Proactive: We identify opportunities for growth and lead others to create the future we envision.

Respect/Win–Win: We treat each other with respect and seek "win-win" relationships with guests, business partners and our communities.

Growth: For Panda to grow, we must each learn and grow. We are humble and open to new ideas as our world is constantly changing.

Great Operations: Great operations is a competitive advantage, both in our restaurants and support center.

Giving: We give our time and resources to support each other and our communities.

PANDA CARES

Panda Cares is a community involvement program that was established by Panda Restaurant Group, Inc. in 1999. Since its inception, Panda Cares has given millions of dollars of donations to numerous non-profit organizations, schools, and hospitals. Panda Cares' purpose is to promote the spirit of giving and establish a caring presence in communities where Panda Restaurant Group's guests and associates live and work. As one of our Panda core values, 'Giving,' states: We give our time and resources to support each other and our communities.

UNLOCKING SHARED LEADERSHIP IN HIGH GROWTH ENVIRONMENTS

Fostering a Culture of Shared Leadership

Developing Vision: From Selling Chinese Food to Inspiring People to Better their Lives

Top executives describe how they have worked persistently to solidify the mission, vision, and values of Panda into daily reality. New employees and visitors to Panda's support center are greeted with a clearly visible sign stating the values of the organization. Yet, the senior team questioned whether employees really understood what those words mean, and whether every part and each and every employee at Panda really understood what Panda's mission and values signify. So, the senior team runs every meeting starting with the mission and Panda's values; as one executive noted, "and an understanding that *that* is the culture that we want to create and maintain here, the rest follows.

M + V = C: Building a Corporate Family

What adjectives best describe Panda? Ask employees and you are likely to hear the following: Dynamic. Conservative. Focused. Relentless. Caring. Committed. Loyal. Frustrated. Passionate. Intelligent. Friendly. Eager. Energetic. Enthusiastic. Enlightening. Opportunistic. Fun. Family. One Zone Vice President of Operations put it this way: "Panda really feels like a family. People care about each other, and people also have a good heart to one other. We create an environment so that you can feel like family, so that you can feel a big part of it all."

In working to continually emphasize shared mission and vision, members of the Panda team have developed creative ways to enact Panda's mission.

As one senior executive pointed out that "M plus V equals C, so our Mission plus our Values equals our Culture. That's what I walk through my new hires with. Because I think we have to tie it all together. Because we've got this mission that talks about selling Chinese food and making money. And then it talks about inspiring people to better their lives."

Others at Panda have focused on the integration of Panda's core values with Steven Covey's *Seven Habits of Highly Effective People* (Covey, 1990) to integrate the focus on developing people into a coherent theme. As another top executive noted, "We've kind of melded the Covey stuff in with it. And I think that all has been a powerful sort of congealing, if you will, of what was here before and really focusing what Panda's philosophy really is behind that." At Panda, employees believe that if you want to become a better businessman or businesswoman, at first you must be a better person. Continual self-improvement is seen as an integral component of both self and employee development. Overall, Panda is a company that walks its mission and talks its mission; that embraces its values and knows that's what defines its culture. Another senior associate commented: "I'm ecstatic to be part of an organization where I can take not only my passion for the tactical job I do, but the passion I have for developing people. I'm able to do that here, because it's taken so seriously."

Communicating Shared Vision to the Right People

The senior team is also strongly aware of the importance of communication of this shared vision, particularly in periods of rapid growth and upheaval. Panda is "really good" about keeping everybody aware of what is happening at all times. According to one top manager, meetings each period let everybody know "where we are financially, what we're doing, how we're doing, how we compare to others. Panda is good about keeping everybody informed. So you feel like you're really a part of the company and not just somebody who comes in, does their time, and leaves."

An important aspect of communicating Panda's shared values and vision is selecting the right people who embrace the company's values. Historically, Andrew Cherng interviews new people wanting to come into the organization, and potential employees are asked to read Covey's *Seven Habits of Highly Effective People* and individually understand how it applies to their own lives. Panda's selection process thus helps new employees understand what mission are they on individually, and how Panda fits in to help them in achieving their mission. In looking for new people, Panda sends a clear message that they do not just want someone who wants to come in and serve food or be an accountant or a marketing manager, but someone who really wants to help Panda on its mission of collective development. New hires clearly understand that is part of their mission as individuals, with an emphasis on what they are trying to learn to enhance themselves as people.

Another manager noted: "They may not know what their mission is today, but at least trying to learn what their mission is and using the Covey stuff to figure out. Their mission may end up not being Panda, but at least there is the desire to learn and to grow and then find that out while they're here."

Admitting Mistakes and Letting Go of the Wrong People

In addition to selecting the right people and emphasizing their roles in developing themselves personally and professionally, letting go of those who are not open to growth and shared leadership is equally important. Particularly in an environment focused on personal growth and facilitating development, it can be hard for leaders to admit they made a mistake in hiring someone and make the difficult decision not to give somebody a longer period of time to change or prove themselves. However, letting go of the wrong people sends a powerful signal that can reinforce the collective vision as well. According to one executive, letting go of one of the senior team who did not embrace Panda's values; "showed that they really respected the people that they have and made a decision in the betterment of everybody."

Emphasis on Open Learning

At Panda, shared leadership is also fostered through an open environment that encourages people to engage one another and work together. As one Zone VP of Operations stated, "One of the things I really like about Panda is you can get to know the CEO of the company if you're a person who just joined the company, or if you're working one of the charity benefits. It doesn't matter. We've got a very open, engaging kind of familial type of feeling going on at Panda, which makes it a great place to be. I think it's really wonderful from that perspective." Panda prides itself on being a continual learning company. Panda values people who keep continually learning and becoming a better and better person, not only as a business, but as an individual whose development becomes an integral component of the business. Hyundai is another company that focuses on learning. See Box 10.2 to see how Mr. Hong, the head of Hyundai H&S promotes learning and shared leadership in his own unique way.

BOX 10.2—SHARED LEADERSHIP AT THE GRASSROOTS LEVEL AT HYUNDAI FOOD SYSTEMS

Craig L. Pearce and Young-Chul Chang

Hyundai Corporation has recently gained prominence on the world stage, largely because of the rapid expansion of their automotive division into North America and other markets. But their prominence is not only due to their rapid expansion but also to the fact that the quality of their automobiles surpasses all other manufacturers, except Porsche, according to a recent J. D. Powers survey.

While their automotive section is highly visible, Hyundai is, in fact, a huge conglomerate, with economic activity in nearly all business sectors. One of the interesting divisions of Hyundai is Hyundai H&S, which was headed by Mr. Hong, Sung Won, and is remarkably successful. We caught up with Mr. Hong to uncover some of the secrets to their success. He boiled it down to two related factors. First, he said, "Everything depends on innovation; we are constantly trying new things." In fact, they are always experimenting with new versions of current offerings—innovating on the margin—as well as creating entirely new products.

How do they encourage appropriate innovation? According to Mr. Hong, it is what he calls "grassroots leadership." Mr. Hong can be described as one who encourages organizational level-jumping: "I like to hear from people at all levels of the organization," says Mr. Hong. He stated that "middle management can sometimes act like a filter. . . . I want to hear from those on the front line." By doing so, Mr. Hong provides a context for the sharing of leadership at the grassroots level and they have leveraged this to great advantage.

So, how does this work in action? The reality is that it is very simply. Mr. Hong has a practice of regularly meeting with front line employees, mostly with those in the research and development area, but also with those in the sales force. According to Mr. Hong, "They are the first ones to hear what our customers want." Clearly, Mr. Hong practices "management by walking around (MBWA)," a term made popular in the 1980s. But more importantly he encourages, "Leadership by Asking Around (LBAA)," by encouraging grassroots leadership from front line employees.

Sharing the lead in organizations can take many forms, and how to do so appropriately depends on one's organizational circumstances. Obviously, Hyundai, and Mr. Hong, provide an alternative model for viewing how to engage the human spirit at work. Perhaps, there is something you can glean from their approach to integrate into your shared leadership model.

UNLOCKING SHARED LEADERSHIP IN HIGH GROWTH ENVIRONMENTS

Cultural Facilitators at Panda

Finding the Right Balance between Work and Play

Hand in hand with the emphasis on continual self-development, employees at Panda work hard. Grounded in the entrepreneurial spirit of the founders, employees at Panda have a "can-do attitude." Attributed to the continually strong influence of the Cherng's, employees display "an immigrant work ethic, promote from within" type of environment. Panda is frequently described by employees as entrepreneurial, dynamic, aggressive, and hard-working. Employees recognize that this aggressive focus could be interpreted in a negative way. But they are also quick to point out that Panda's focus on proactively building relationships, combined with an aggressive and even demanding work ethic, creates an environment where employees are both stretched and challenged to do their best and also supported and encouraged to develop personally to achieve that best. One associate noted, "Panda employees work hard and play hard. Both have a significant meaning, meaning we work but we play. We have fun while we work."

While the work ethic dates back to the roots of the firm, they have crystallized this core cultural value into the predominant symbol of the company: the pyramid. They visibly captured the importance of these initial and deeply rooted values in the People, Guest, and Financial pyramid. In addition, employees and the senior team have melded this emphasis with the emphasis on Stephen Covey' *Seven Principles of Highly Effective People.* Thus, they have successfully balanced the hard-working, entrepreneurial roots of the founders with an emphasis on providing a fun supportive environment to support the demands of the job. According to one executive, employees recognize that this balance "has been a powerful sort of congealing, if you will, of what was here before and really focusing what Panda's philosophy really is behind that."

Balancing Collaboration and Clear Accountability

In addition to balancing work and play, Panda management role models a commitment to supporting one another. Senior managers regularly go to the store level and talk to employees, talk to general managers one-on-one, try to understand and feel the morale at the field level, and also try to understand what people need and what people are looking for. According to one Zone VP, managers regularly "try to check the temperature of the field and what's needed, what do we do well, what we didn't do right as management so that we can be very quick to make repairs." Tracing back to the "can-do" attitude of the organization, employees are encouraged to proactively ask what they can do to support one another, and what they can do to get in on a project. The emphasis on supporting one another is a key theme in the senior team as well. Another senior executive pointed out that this support helps the team strive "to see how close knit and in pace and interlaced this leadership team can be, is just going to be, if we are the fireworks that are set off, then we're going to ignite the rest of the organization."

Panda employees are also encouraged to look outside of the function that they work in for support and opportunities for collaboration. The focus is on internal people as the fundamental talent base, and employees are encouraged to allow their passions and desires to grow and develop, wherever they might lead. The result is often very blurry lines between functional areas. Accountability is clear, but people are actively encouraged to proactively seek answers to questions, explore new ideas, and collaborate with others regardless of their position in the organizational structure.

However, employees emphasize that Panda is also pragmatic and results oriented, which facilitates shared leadership around common problems and opportunities. Closely related to their hardworking approach, having clear metrics for success and areas of accountability helps create an atmosphere of flexibility where employees can work together to reach goals. As one Zone VP stated, "we have accountability, responsibility in each level in who reports to who. I think it's very, very clear and very rare."

Unlocking Shared Leadership in High Growth Environments

Structuring Opportunities for Shared Leadership

Shared leadership is a consistent theme that is clearly evident in the structure and process of the Team Panda, a salient signal from the most visible level of the organization that shared leadership is a critical piece underlying Panda's continued success. The senior team holds weekly team meetings around long-range planning, with one or both Co-CEOs presiding over the meetings. The leadership in these more structured team meetings took a variety of functions, including checking and setting the agenda, monitoring the process, facilitating discussions, making decisions, and ultimately cutting off discussions if the team needed to move on. In team meetings, the formal leader does not try to dominate the meeting, but focuses on facilitating discussions, making sure the team gets done what it would like to get done, and structuring some of the agenda. In other words, the formal leader makes sure that things are progressing on track or makes decisions where they need to be made, or cutting off discussion if the team needs to move on.

As a result, team members are free to contribute their strengths and begin to coalesce into a real team. One top manager described the team as follows: "I would say, you know, we're pretty cohesive. We get along well. It's a fun group, some good personalities. It's a passionate group that really loves what they're doing. It's energetic as well. It's a fairly young group. And I would say it's a pretty aggressive group in both the things that we want to accomplish and the agenda we're trying to move forward for the company. So a very forward-leaning senior team. I think it's a smart group and a talented group but also a group that is very humble and respectful and works well together." Thomas Keller, the famous chef also believes in structuring situations for sharing leadership. Box 10.3 examines how they shared the lead at the French Laundry to create world-class cuisine.

BOX 10.3—SHARING THE MENU—
THOMAS KELLER AND THE FRENCH LAUNDRY

Christina L. Wassenaar

A typical chef rules their kitchen. They design the menu and the theme, the style of cuisine, they select the vendors, the ingredients, and how they are presented to the customers in their final preparation. Traditionally, it is the job of the chef de cuisine, the sous chef, or any of the rest of the kitchen and wait staff to simply *repeat* the vision of the head chef, but never to interpret, improvise and never, ever to create.

This is not the case in the land of Chef Thomas Keller. In his kitchens, each part of a growing group of restaurants scattered around the United States, he takes a different tack, one of vision and empowerment. He sets the vision: that of extremely high quality ingredients and preparations, based on seasonal and local organic ingredients, served in both tradition-al and innovative ways in memorable settings. Then he hires people who can execute that vision with little hands-on guidance from him. He states, "Cooking is a simple equation: product and execution. If you have quality product and people who are going to execute it; bringing the two together, a strong team with a common goal and building relationships with suppliers you've got great food."

He goes on to say, "Chefs have a new responsibility. No longer are there just one restaurant, one menu. This means we have to hand down to our younger chefs the opportunities that we have. That can mean writing a book, or creating a menu, or sourcing a new sort of supply. They have a determina-tion to, everyday evolve their work a little better than the day before."

By managing his kitchen in this way he is able to immediately accomplish several things. First, he is able to hire some of the most talented, up and coming people who want to learn from him yet who are also interested in developing their own flavors in their cooking. Secondly, these people will understand very clearly how the environment that Chef Keller creates is dif-ferent. Because they recognize this difference they are more committed to the overall vision and success of the French Laundry Group, because, at the end of the day, they are a foundational part of their overall success.

Balancing Shared Decision Making and Making Decisions

Consistent with a shared leadership approach, decisions in the senior team are primarily consensus based. Issues are discussed among the whole senior team, exploring pros and cons, remaining doubts and potential con-straints. After allowing for dialogue, a recommendation is frequently made by whoever is in charge of presenting that particular issue. The team then either agrees or disagrees, but decisions are typically made by consensus. There's not usually a vote *per se*. According to one executive, "It's more, do we all think this is it—is there kind of a majority that feels like we agree with the recommendation on that particular issue."

Shared Leadership in the Senior Team

When asked to choose adjectives to describe the senior team, descriptors are: Fair. United. Intellectual. Diverse. Cohesive. Specialized. Fun. Collegial. Competitive. Intelligent. Experienced. Everybody on the team is described as a hard worker and very competitive. The team is also evolving, comprising a blend of members that have been around for more than a decade, as well as some newer members that have come into the organization within the last few years. More recently, one of the new members of the top management team noted that members are "still figuring out how to work effectively together as a team as we go through situations that are both positive and challenging. And so we're learning about each other as the company's moving at really a fairly quick pace."

In addition, they emphasized that a good idea poorly executed has little or no benefit. But a mediocre idea, exceptionally executed, means a lot. In order to get people to execute at the highest levels, employees need to have a stake or an ownership interest in what they're trying to accomplish. And so with that in mind, formal leaders must allow more open and fluid communication around how to get from Point A to Point B. So everyone has an influence, has an impact on implementation, and has ownership in what the ultimate objective is, leading to people who want to contribute discretionary effort to make sure implementation is effective.

Employees at Panda recognize that, as with most things in life, there are a number of different ways you can get to the right solution or outcome. As a senior executive pointed out, there is often no one right idea, but three or five right ideas. In this model, the 'right' idea is the one of those three or five where the group says, "I'm all in. I'm going to make it work," and then works tirelessly and with full focus and engagement to make it effective. In shared leadership, the formal leaders often let the group form around the solution and then move forward.

At Panda, formal leaders also emphasize "picking their spots." Leadership does not involve micromanaging in any sense, but by the same token it's also not abdicating responsibility. As one Zone VP described it, "I was a transactional type of a person before, and now I'm dealing with people, it's more of a transformational type of a role. And we engage in debates from time to time on topics that we don't see eye to eye on. And that's fine." Shared leadership also involves looking for opportunities to delegate, so that other people can gain skills and experience and grow and develop. And what that does for the organization is build "a bunch of people that can think for themselves and make decisions for themselves" so that formal leaders can focus on other things that need attention.

Promoting Mutual Influence within the Team

In addition to recognizing occasions when formal leader decisions are necessary, effective shared leadership also involves actively fostering mutual influence among various members of the senior team. For example, one member of the senior team described the process through which the team discussed how Panda allocates bonuses. After some pretty significant changes to managerial bonuses had been made, one senior executive proposed some additional tweaks to the system. According to him, "another member of the team responded, 'I don't think that's a good idea. My experience has been you need to get a little stability first. You're trying to move a little too fast.' And that's one of those situations where I just have a lot of respect for her and said, 'Okay.' I can see both sides of it. My tendency is to move. But if your experience says that that's going to cause more damage than what I'm willing to accept, okay, let's back off a little bit." This type of back and forth, mutual influence among team members is described as a "pretty typical" kind of interaction. Decisions are made through mutual influence, constructive conflict, and bringing issues to table for discussion.

Shared Leadership Doesn't Always Happen In Team Meetings

Overall, the senior team functions within this consensus model, with clear lines of accountability linked back to functional areas. If the issue is a functional issue, the functional head is most likely to make a recommendation, invite input, and move forward from there. On issues of more company-wide goal setting, the team operates very much from a consensus model, but the Co-CEOs are recognized as the formal leaders with the authority to exercise a veto right to say, yes, these are all important, but we really want us to focus on these three or four things. One of the senior executives noted, "Because we are all working on a set of goals for the senior team for the year, there's a lot of interaction week in and out among different members of the senior team around collaborating toward achieving those goals." Typically, there is some pre-work and outside discussion involved in putting together information for the senior team prior to it going on the agenda.

In this manner, mutual influence and shared leadership can appear somewhat 'ad hoc' in some respects and extremely fluid as well. At Panda, "75% of the action" happens outside of that senior team meeting. That's not to say that there aren't other members of the senior team involved in a particular project, but projects come back for general information sharing and feedback and then go back out to a sub-team, which may include one or two senior management members on it. And in each one of those instances the subject matter expert works with one other person from the senior team, depending on what needs to be done. And then may come back to the larger group for comment and feedback. As a result, it is not always clearly determined ahead of time who is going to be involved in a decision. If something needs to happen before the next weekly meeting, it tends to be determined more "by who is available" as members are willing to step in and take over when they can.

Shared Leadership Necessitates Trust to Ask For Help

In a similar vein, senior team members reported a strong willingness to help each other out. Team members point out that this necessitates a fair amount of trust and mutual respect in order to work smoothly. For example, team members can feel as if asking for help involves opening one-self up for vulnerabilities, or can be perceived as stepping on another team member's toes. Between team members who have higher levels of trust, employees are more likely to be able to give and receive honest feedback, ask for help, and take risks that might involve questions of turf or account-ability. For many employees, this level of trust occurs only through spend-ing more time with one another. In addition, the use of off-site senior team meetings helps facilitate team members getting to know each other better and building trust and appreciation for what is important to the collective group. But all of these processes take time.

However, this process of building trust is critical to implementing shared leadership in times of rapid growth. In addition, high levels of trust can be the difference between a team of individually bright people and proven leaders who fail to coalesce. One executive pointed out "that just takes more time working together, more opportunity to really to build trust. But we haven't always had the time or the time is not invested to really get us there to where we all trust each other. I don't think there's distrust. Don't get me wrong. I really don't think there's distrust in any single team member that I've noticed. But that's different than really truly building a trusting relationship that you can then call friend. And you know, I've had to learn over time that I have to let things go and trust that other people could do it as good as I can, or sometimes even better than I can because that's their niche."

As trusting relationships have developed over time, members of the se-nior team can also look to each other for multiple examples of what type of a leader they each aspire to be. In addition, teammates become learning material, helping each member to see how they can individually develop different aspects of the shared leadership model. One senior manager summed it up this way: "To me, it's a continuous path of growth. And if I stop growing, then shame on me. I have so many people who are respon-sible for me; I have to continue to grow to continue to teach. And so I learn from them as they're growing. I'm watching them and I'm growing. So I think the team has been an important role model exercise; because they bring so many different sides to a leader. And I can take from each one of them a little something, the best of each one of them and aspire to be the best of all of that." Especially in a company with growing pains and on a path of rapid expansion that Panda has experienced, employees recognize how critical it is to make sure that somebody is making sure that the processes flow effectively and efficiently, and that managers rather than the critical individual contributors are collaborating with other managers.

Allowing Mistakes and Avoiding Blame

Within the senior team, there is also the recognition at Panda that employees must be allowed to make mistakes and managers cannot worry too much about those mistakes without compromising the process of shared leadership. One executive reflected: "I allow my folks to make mistakes and learn from those mistakes rather than to direct them away from them. Because people let me make my mistakes, and that's what got me to where I am. . . . The big epiphany for me at Panda is that it takes more than being a great leader. It takes more than being a great manager. It is critical to have the ability to teach either through example or more directly."

Given Panda's hardworking, can-do work ethic, leaders have to be extremely sensitive to how they wield their influence. "If you say at Panda, "I'd like the sky to be red today," there could be hundreds of people out there trying to figure out how to do that. They will try and make something happen. So you have to be careful with the words that you use and when you say you want something, need something, desire some change, because they'll go out and they'll do it." So, influence is shared, and mistakes are recognized as inevitable. One executive emphasized, "Let's not put blame on anybody. Let's just fix the problems. Let's find the solutions to the problems." Through working together collaboratively, members of the senior team have managed to solve a lot of problems, resulting in a more cohesive team.

Making Sure All Voices Are Heard

Finally, shared leadership involves making sure that the voices of each team member are solicited and heard. Recognizing that part of developing others is helping them feel comfortable expressing ideas, team members try to be cognizant of the effects of jumping too quickly into a conversation and immediately starting to express opinions. Trying to draw others out and get them to engage in the conversation provides a big opportunity for team members to engage in more dynamic conversations in which all associates can be heard.

MOVING FORWARD

Continual Development and the Evolving Panda Story

According to one senior manager, "the best thing about Panda is kind of that sense that we're on a mission, that we're all part of something bigger than each of us individually, that we're all here to be part of the Panda story and to see Panda Express go from now $1B to $2B and beyond. And that that will provide a lot of growth opportunities for everybody here as well as financial opportunities. And I think just that sense that we're on this mission together and it's a worthy cause. So I think that makes people very passionate and inspired about what they're doing."

Overall, Panda is an organization that is "really, really committed to improving and developing people, whether it's through the Covey stuff or whether it's through other organizational development activities." There is a collective sense that not only does Panda want to achieve its mission and its vision, but it wants to help each individual achieve their own mission and vision, and that the organization is committed to putting resources behind that. Employees at Panda recognize that it is "pretty rare when you find a group of people that are that focused on achieving a mission and aren't being distracted by politics or petty maneuvering."

Consistently, Panda employees recognize the importance of their history, the legacy of the founders, and their ongoing "story" in developing a path forward. As one executive noted "as we create and write our new story and the new journey to take us to the new place, it requires some things that some employees may have a hard time agreeing with or accepting." Within an organization focused on continual individual and organizational development, this is a challenging expectation that employees are well equipped to meet.

According to another executive, "It's an amazing organization. It's one of those great American success stories of starting with one restaurant and now having a thousand." Yet, another executive noted, Panda is "somewhat of a unique animal just because of the very strong personalities and interests involved in that business, and the cultural differences that exist within our organization. And so it's always a place where there's learning and growth. And I think we're sort of gassing up right now, which [is] a good place to be in terms of getting stronger as a leadership team, this inner team, because our opportunities continue to grow and we need to become more effective at dealing with them to reach great solutions fast. That's what we're working on."

In addition, despite all of its success, Panda is still a very humble organization. Grounded in its historical roots is Panda's legacy of a modest, hard-working, and proactive approach. Yet, this humility does not restrict the potential for continued high growth and expansion. One executive summed it up this way: "There's still a lot of room to grow. There's still tons of runway left for Panda. I can't imagine a more exciting place to be in the restaurant industry. Not only is it a great concept and a great growth story, but just a great organization and philosophy."

The latest strategic move at Panda is the creation of the University of Panda. The vision for the university is for it to be a place to acculturate new associates into the Panda-way, while also providing ongoing development for managers throughout their entire careers at Panda. Founders Andrew and Peggy Cherng really want to have an organization where people are inspired to better their lives. It is such a simple recipe for success.

CHAPTER TAKEAWAYS

1. Focus on creating a vibrant organizational culture that consists of complimentary values. Organizational culture is the only real source of, long-term sustainable competitive advantage.
2. Forget about pointing fingers and identifying blame for problems. That is a short-term, person centered approach. Rather, focus on identifying root causes of problems and solving them. That is the long-term, organization centered approach.
3. Create a sense of purpose that transcends the simple bottom line. People want to be involved in something that is more meaningful that just making money. They want to make a meaningful impact. This reduces turnover and increases commitment.
4. Even with shared leadership there is a role for hierarchy. Shared leadership does not mean abdication of responsibility. On the contrary, hierarchical leaders need to lead even more, when engaging shared leadership processes.

REFERENCE

Covey, S. 1990. *The seven habits of highly effective people.* New York, NY: Fireside.

CONCLUDING THOUGHTS ON SHARED LEADERSHIP

Craig L. Pearce and Charles C. Manz

In this book, we have taken a practical, hands-on, epic leadership journey. We have seen the inner workings of dozens of organizations. We have seen what sets them apart; what gives them distinction; what provides them sustainability and strategic advantage: In every case, albeit implemented idiosyncratically, it was their focus on extreme empowerment and palpable engagement in shared leadership.

OUR LEADERSHIP JOURNEY LOGBOOK

Below we briefly recap our leadership journey, then we identify the overarching leadership lessons on which to focus for moving your organization forward on your shared leadership expedition. We explored many different types of organizations in this book ranging from large to small, from for profit to not-for-profit, from US-based to international and from manufacturing to service.

Our sojourn in the service sector revealed the secrets to the success of such organizations as Southwest Airlines—the only continuously profitable major airline in the United States. They are very clear about it: They trust their people to do "whatever it takes to make this organization more

Share, Don't Take the Lead, pages 163–169
Copyright © 2014 by Information Age Publishing

successful": After all, they put that phrase as the last line in all of their job descriptions. We also, albeit briefly, visited Swiss Air where we found shared leadership a critical component in flight safety. On the dimmer side we found a dearth of leadership at United Airlines, which probably explains their lack luster performance.

Beyond the service sector we ventured into manufacturing where we revealed the inner workings of organizations like W. L. Gore & Associates and Herman Miller. Both organizations focus on how to unleash the creative potential of employees. Both are highly successful: Gore, in the application of material science and Miller in the production of office furniture. Most likely, every reader of this book has used their products. Perhaps you are even now sitting on a Herman Miller chair, wearing clothing made from Gortex®, Gore's most famous product. We also examined Behlen Manufacturing, whose humble beginnings in Columbus, Nebraska now extend around the globe because Tony Raimondo and team treat all of their employees as "partners in progress" and they are an exemplar of the absolute cutting edge of leadership practice.

We also examined the restaurant industry. Here we primarily focused on Panda Restaurant Group—owner of the Panda Express chain of quick service Asian restaurants, in addition to the Panda Inn and Habatchisan restaurant chains. Panda's mission is to "Deliver exceptional Asian dining experiences by building an organization where people are inspired to better their lives." Sounds like a lofty ideal. But they mean it. And they have done so, in profound ways. The first author knows this particular organization intimately, as he directed their executive education program to groom rising stars for more than a decade. The Panda Express chain has grown from one store in 1983 to more than 1,600 today, all the while providing opportunity, both financial and personal, to their associates. Their secret? Shared leadership. They actively engage people. They desire people to succeed in all dimensions of their lives. And the current Co-CEOs, Andrew and Peggy Cherng are working diligently to ensure Panda makes a positive contribution to society. At the high end of the restaurant spectrum, we visited The French Laundry, where world famous chef Thomas Keller minces no words about it: It is by sharing leadership in the kitchen that they have reached the pinnacle of the culinary world.

Moving to the non-profit sector, we delved into the inner workings of such organizations as Alcoholics Anonymous and the Braille Institute of America. Both are significantly voluntary organizations. So how do such organizations motivate people to lead? It is all about purpose. Providing people with a meaningful purpose is a highly energizing force. At the Braille Institute is it is about helping the visually impaired. At Alcoholics Anonymous it is about breaking the cycle of addiction that undermines human potential. If we could extract a mere sliver of what makes these organizations so successful and apply it to the business sector our world would be transformed.

Shifting to the medical sector, we dove deep into the University of Maryland Shock Trauma Center—The ER. Here again we saw leadership in action, but the stakes were much higher. There life hangs in the balance. Yet the common cord through each of these organizations was shared leadership. Sure it played out differently in the divergent contexts. At the ER we witnessed the dynamic shift between hierarchical and shared leadership, depending on the skills of those involved and the specifics of the case at hand. So it isn't a choice between hierarchical and shared leadership, it is a matter of which to engage and how to dynamically move between them. We made brief pit stops at Madonna Rehabilitation Hospital and Loma Linda University Medical Center, where their CEOs Marsha Lommel and Ruthita Fike, respectively, are creating some of the most engaged workforces anywhere by boldly sharing leadership. We also saw some exciting new medical research coming out of Switzerland which clearly demonstrates that when doctors share leadership with nurses they enhance their ability to save lives—how much more important can the message become that sharing leadership is a management imperative?

While most of our organizations were based in the United States, many have far flung operations overseas. Look at Alcoa, a true global player. And how do they coordinate their operations that span the world? First they make extensive use of technology and virtual teams. But what is critical to understand is how those teams function. What distinguishes the best teams is how seamlessly they deploy shared leadership: It is the glue that binds them together and it is the social process that keeps things moving 24–7. Complimentary to our findings at Alcoa, we saw similar patterns in the virtual teams deployed at Bosch, the giant German conglomerate.

Other examples were specifically based in other countries. For example, Hyundai H&S, a division of the enormous South Korean chaebol, Hyundai, headed by Mr. Sung Won Hong encourages what he calls "grass roots leadership" to ensure that the firm stays innovative and at the leading edge of their industry. Importantly, the South Korean culture is known for deference to hierarchical power, which inhibits the development of shared leadership. With that said, another Korean firm, Yuhan-Kimberly, vaulted to the number one paper products company in Korea, with the leadership of Mr. H. K. Moon, specifically because they minimized hierarchical differences and developed shared leadership. They take the concept so far that they have even tried to help their competitors develop shared leadership by opening their books, so to speak, so that others can learn from them. Moving from Korea to Afghanistan, we explored how they are rebuilding the educational infrastructure in this beleaguered nation. What we found was an inspiring story of both caring and sharing. These remarkable people have come together, in spite of the mortal danger and have created a cohesive network of social support and influence that is transforming the lives of millions.

OVERARCHING LESSONS FOR SHARED LEADERSHIP

So what are the overarching lessons that we can take away from our epic journey? The lessons, as we reflect on the various chapters and sidebars that capture the essence of the organizations profiled in this book are captured in Figure 11.1—what we call the Shared Leadership Diamond—and span four major categories: (1) individual level lessons; (2) group/team level lessons; (3) organization level lessons; and (4) human resources practices lessons. Below we detail these, providing a comprehensive guide to action for the development of shared leadership in your organization.

The Shared Leadership Diamond

Key Lessons for Leveraging Shared Leadership for Success in Your Organization
at the Levels of the: (1) Individual; (2) Group/Team; (3) Organization;
and (4) Human Resource Practices

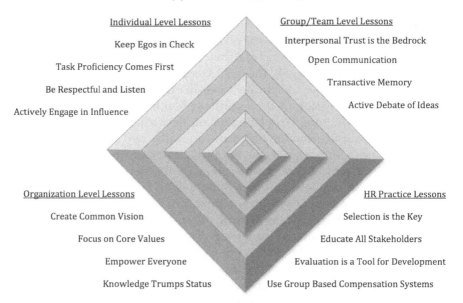

Individual Level Lessons
Keep Egos in Check
Task Proficiency Comes First
Be Respectful and Listen
Actively Engage in Influence

Group/Team Level Lessons
Interpersonal Trust is the Bedrock
Open Communication
Transactive Memory
Active Debate of Ideas

Organization Level Lessons
Create Common Vision
Focus on Core Values
Empower Everyone
Knowledge Trumps Status

HR Practice Lessons
Selection is the Key
Educate All Stakeholders
Evaluation is a Tool for Development
Use Group Based Compensation Systems

Figure 11.1   The Shared Leadership Diamond

Individual Level Lessons

If shared leadership is to succeed the individuals involved first need to keep their egos in check. This is not an easy task, especially for smart people. Yet, setting egos aside allows for the focus to change from the "I" to the "we" and in today's complex world the overwhelming majority of work product produced requires the collaboration of individuals. As such, the individuals involved in sharing leadership also must have the knowledge, skills and abilities (KSAs) for their tasks. Otherwise, we would simply have the proverbial blind leading the blind. Beyond task related KSAs, however, individuals must have keen listening skills if they are to effectively share the lead with others. Additionally, they also must show respect for others' ideas and perspectives. Finally, they must be proactive leaders and prepared to engage in active influence of others. No matter how smart a particular person is, without the gumption to stand up and lead, when the group needs the knowledge of the individual at hand, shared leadership will fail. Accordingly, these are the highlights of the lessons for shared leadership, derived from this book, to apply at the individual level.

Group/Team Level Lessons

Trust is the bedrock for the development of shared leadership in groups and teams. Emerging research from neuro-economics has even demonstrated that trust can be traced to the economic success of societies. As groups and teams are the basic building blocks of larger social entities they are the place where trust must be built. And part of building trust is having open communication because it helps to facilitate the ebb a flow of knowledge within the group and keeps people from second-guessing one another when it comes to the important decisions that inevitably arise. This brings us to what scholars call transactive memory—being aware of who has the most relevant KSAs in which topics. Transactive memory is critical to having leadership transitions to the most appropriate person(s) for any given task. It is all well and good to say that leadership should be shared but it is imperative that the correct person be leading at the correct time, i.e., based on their knowledge of the task at hand, and not just based on personality or some other trivial factor. So failing well developed transactive memory, how does one help ensure identification of the correct leader for the given moment? This is where desire to debate ideas enters the picture. If group and team norms stress the constructive challenge of each others' ideas research clearly demonstrates that this type of exchange drives creativity and innovation. As such, there are several specific shared leadership lessons from this book to apply at the group/team level.

Organization Level Lessons

A common vision and purpose helps to unify the organization and direct energy toward super-ordinate goals. Having said that, most organizational leaders over-estimate the degree to which vision and purpose are truly shared. Engaging others in creating the vision is one way to help ensure that the vision is actually shared but ongoing testing, prodding and assessment of shared vision should be part of the organizational toolkit in order to facilitate shared leadership. Similarly, focus on creating shared values is also critical. In the end, shared cultural values are the only long-term source of competitive advantage that is not easily copied.

It should be clear by now that we advocate empowering everyone, at least to some degree. Nearly every single person is capable of taking on some leadership responsibility and positively contributing to organizational success. In this regard, knowledge should always trump status. Encourage those with the most relevant knowledge to provide leadership, not simply those with the highest status. And this means looking beyond artificial borders to tap broad sources of inputs. Often this means looking outside the organization to involve customers, suppliers and other important stakeholders in the leadership of the organization. While this can sometimes be uncomfortable it can also be quite rewarding.

Human Resource Practice Lessons

Selection is perhaps the single most important thing ever to be done. The issue here is looking for person/job and person/organization fit. Different organizational circumstances call for different individual attributes. However, most organizations do a pitiful job of selecting people. Two organizations in this book are certainly among the very best at this task—Southwest Airlines and W. L. Gore. Learn from their examples.

Beyond selection, one needs to strongly engage in ongoing education, training and development for all employees, not just those in formal leadership positions. Similarly, evaluation needs to be used as a tool for development and intervention—360s are one potential mechanism to employ—not just a way to beat up people. Compensation is another oft overlooked mechanism for leveraging leadership talent. Here the issue involves the appropriate use of group-based compensation, such as gainsharing, that encourages the sharing of leadership across organizational lines. Together, these sets of tools equip you to tackle the majority of leadership challenges that crop up, from time to time, in organizations.

WHERE DO WE GO FROM HERE?

We have witnessed a substantial increase in the utilization of team-based structures in organizations in recent years. In large part, this change is a response to an increasingly challenging environment that requires enhanced organizational flexibility. However, as many leaders are quite aware, true teamwork poses many challenges. It is precisely because of the challenges of working in a team-based environment that we must question if our traditional models of leadership are still appropriate. In this book, we have attempted to clarify an alternate form of leadership—shared leadership—that helps to provide insight into leadership in the age of knowledge work. And we have provided many impressive examples of its successful application. Will the implementation of shared leadership be painful? For many organizations the unfortunate answer is yes. The alternative, however, of suboptimal organizations and overburdened leaders is ultimately even more painful.

Are we approaching the dusk of the hierarchical leadership? Unambiguously no. It is not a matter of choosing between hierarchical leadership and shared leadership. On the contrary, the issues are: (1) when is leadership most appropriately shared; (2) how does one develop shared leadership; and (3) how does one shift between hierarchical and shared leadership. By addressing these issues in your own organization, you will move toward the more appropriate practice of leadership in the age of knowledge work. And these are the questions we have addressed throughout this book. We hope you have found the chapters to vividly illustrate how shared leadership can and should work. We also documented the primary challenges to its implementation. Together we have taken an epic journey through 21 real organizations that are reaping the rewards of building shared leadership cultures. Is it time for your organization to begin its own shared leadership journey, with all the potential payoffs it offers for all involved? Only you can answer that question.

ABOUT THE AUTHORS

Craig L. Pearce, Ph.D., is the Director of the Deloitte Leadership Institute at Ozyegin University in Istanbul, Turkey. He was formerly the Dean of the School of Business and Entrepreneurship at the American University of Nigeria. Before that he was the Donald Clifton Chair in Leadership and the Director of the Institute for Innovative Leadership at the University of Nebraska-Lincoln and previously he worked with Peter Drucker at the Peter F. Drucker and Masatoshi Ito School of Management. He has pioneered the development of shared leadership scholarship and practice. His work has appeared in top journals, is widely cited, has spawned countless doctoral dissertations across the globe, *and* has received widespread acclaim in the practitioner community—including a feature article in the *Wall Street Journal*. He has received many awards for his work including the Ascendant Scholar Award, the Asia Pacific HR Leadership Award and an award from the Center for Creative Leadership for his work on shared leadership. His book, *Shared Leadership: Reframing the Hows and Whys of Leadership*, is published by Sage Publications. His most recent book, *The Drucker Difference*, is published by McGraw-Hill, and has been reprinted in Chinese, German, Indonesian, Japanese, Korean, Portuguese, Spanish and Russian. He is a co-founder of an agricultural biotechnology company. He is an active keynote speaker and consultant to organizations—his clients have included such organizations as American Express, British Bakeries, the Central Intelligence Agency of the USA, Credit Europe Bank, Fujitsu, Land Rover, the Metropolitan Water District of Southern California, Nielsen Marketing, Panda Express, Rayovac, Rover Group, SmartScan and Serono, among many others.

Share, Don't Take the Lead, pages 171–172
Copyright © 2014 by Information Age Publishing

Charles C. Manz, Ph.D., is a speaker, consultant, and best-selling business author. He holds the Charles and Janet Nirenberg Chair of Business Leadership in the Isenberg School of Management at the University of Massachusetts. His work has been featured on radio and television and in *The Wall Street Journal, Fortune, U.S. News & World Report, Success, Psychology Today, Fast Company* and several other national publications. He received the prestigious Marvin Bower Fellowship at the Harvard Business School that is "awarded for outstanding achievement in research and productivity, influence, and leadership in business scholarship." He earned a Ph.D. in Business, with an emphasis in Organizational Behavior and Psychology, from The Pennsylvania State University and MBA and B.A. degrees from Michigan State University. He is the author or co-author of over 200 articles and scholarly papers and more than 20 books including the bestsellers *Business Without Bosses: How Self-Managing Teams Are Building High-Performing Companies*, the Stybel-Peabody prize winning *SuperLeadership: Leading Others to Lead Themselves, The Leadership Wisdom of Jesus: Practical Lessons For Today* (3 editions), *The Power of Failure: 27 Ways to Turn Life's Setbacks Into Success* and Foreword Magazine best book-of-the-year Gold Award winner in the self-help category *Emotional Discipline: The Power to Choose How You Feel.* Dr. Manz has served as a consultant for many organizations, including 3M, Ford, Motorola, Xerox, the Mayo Clinic, Procter & Gamble, General Motors, American Express, Allied Signal, Unisys, Josten's Learning, Banc One, the American Hospital Association, the American College of Physician Executives, the U.S. and Canadian governments, and many others.

Henry P. Sims, Jr., Ph.D. is Professor Emeritus of Management and Organization at the Robert H. Smith School of Business, University of Maryland-College Park. He earned his doctorate from the College of Business, Michigan State University. His area of research is leadership and teams. He has published seven books including the bestsellers *Business Without Bosses: How Self-Managing Teams Are Building High-Performing Companies*, the Stybel-Peabody prize winning *SuperLeadership: Leading Others to Lead Themselves*, and over 130 articles in such journals as *Journal of Applied Psychology, Academy of Management Journal, and Administrative Science Quarterly*. He has served as a consultant to both industry and government.

CPSIA information can be obtained
at www.ICGtesting.com
Printed in the USA
BVHW042123180119
538225BV00008B/49/P